DATE DUE

OCT 3 0 2013	
JAN 3 0 2014	

EXECUTIVE FUNCTION AND CHILD DEVELOPMENT

A Norton Professional Book

Executive Function and Child Development

Marcie Yeager
Daniel Yeager

W. W. NORTON & COMPANY
New York • London

For information about permission to reproduce selections from
this book, write to
Permissions, W. W. Norton & Company, Inc., 500 Fifth Avenue,
New York, NY 10110

For information about special discounts for bulk purchases,
please contact W. W. Norton
Special Sales at specialsales@wwnorton.com or 800-233-4830

Manufacturing by Quad Graphics, Fairfield
Book design by Bytheway Publishing Services
Production manager: Leeann Graham

Library of Congress Cataloging-in-Publication Data

Yeager, Marcie.
    Executive function and child development / Marcie Yeager,
Daniel Yeager.
        p. cm. − (A Norton professional book)
    Includes bibliographical references and index.
    ISBN 978-0-393-70764-9 (hbk.)
    1. Self-control in children.   2. Executive functions
(Neuropsychology)   3. Child psychology.   4. Child
development.   I. Yeager, Marcie.   II. Yeager, Daniel.   III. Title.
    BF723.S25Y43 2013
    155.4'1825−dc23   2012036051

ISBN: 978-0-393-70764-9

W. W. Norton & Company, Inc., 500 Fifth Avenue,
New York, N.Y. 10110
www.wwnorton.com

W. W. Norton & Company Ltd., Castle House, 75/76 Wells Street,
London W1T 3QT

1 2 3 4 5 6 7 8 9 0

To our parents:
Joanne and Jim Fields
Betsy and Willy Yeager

To our children:
Rebekah and Jesse

Contents

PART III INTERVENTIONS THAT SUPPORT EXECUTIVE FUNCTION

Acknowledgments

OUR YOUNG CLIENTS COME TO our office for guidance, for help, for healing, for therapeutic play. They also, unbeknownst to them, come as teachers. They have taught us many valuable lessons over the years, and have wonderfully touched and enriched our lives. We are most appreciative.

We want to express our gratitude to Deborah Malmud (vice president of W. W. Norton & Company and director of Norton Professional Books) for approaching us about this project and steering us through the initial stages. This book would not exist had it not been for her faith in us, her encouragement, and her guidance. She and her colleagues at Norton Professional Books have been patient, professional, perceptive, and a delight to work with.

Preface

IN OUR CHILD AND FAMILY counseling practice, we get phone calls daily from parents seeking solutions to problems like these:

My son doesn't listen. It's like what I tell him goes in one ear and out the other. I get so angry with him and end up yelling at him. Then I feel guilty. Maybe he can't help himself.

Every day it's a struggle to get my daughter ready for school in the morning and to get homework done and to do just about anything. She needs ten times the attention and energy that my other kids need. She's 10 and my 4-year-old needs less supervision than she does. I'm exhausted. Why is she so different from the others?

Once my son gets upset, there is no way to reach him; it's a meltdown and we just have to let it run its course. Everyone in the family walks on eggshells around him because we don't want to set him off. But we have to live our lives. We've tried so many things and nothing seems to help. What are we doing wrong?

With our daughter, we've tried every kind of reward, every kind of punishment. She always promises she'll do better. But the next time it is the same behavior all over again.

What all of these children have in common is difficulty with self-regulation. Unlike their peers, they are unable to bring their behavior in line with expectations that others have for them. In fact, they are unable to bring their behavior in line with their own intentions about how they should behave. Their behavior is puzzling to their parents, to their teachers, and even to themselves.

As mental health professionals who are daily involved in helping children like these, we too have puzzled over their problems with self-regulation. Over many years of practice, we have come to a much better understanding of these difficulties, drawing on three sources of information:

- Theories of executive function, particularly the writings of Russell Barkley.
- Theories of child development, particularly those of Lev Vygotsky.
- The field of play therapy, where we have found professional support and encouragement for our innate faith in the power of play to help all children grow and learn.

Combining what we have learned about executive function and child development and encouraged by the exchange of information with play therapy colleagues, we have developed playful interventions to help children achieve better self-regulation. We have put together a handbook (*Simon Says Pay Attention: Help for Children With ADHD*) as a way to share some of these interventions with other therapists. We have also taught these interventions at conferences across the country. When Deborah Malmud of W.W. Norton Professional Books asked whether we'd be interested in writing a book about executive function and child development, we jumped at the opportunity. The understanding that we have gained has enriched our practice and we hope it will do the same for other clinicians.

We hope that this book may also be useful to parents, teachers, and pediatricians. We know that many of them are looking for alternative methods of helping children who struggle with self-regulation. When families come to our office, they have often already tried one or all of the three treatment interventions (behavior management, accommodations, and medication) typically advised for children with self-regulation difficulties. While those interventions are often successful, they are not universally so, and sometimes a different approach may be needed. And even when they are successful, we have found that our approach, which directly engages the child as an active partner, adds a fourth dimension to treatment that has long-term benefits.

EXECUTIVE FUNCTION AND CHILD DEVELOPMENT

PART I

Understanding Executive Function

CHAPTER ONE

Self-Regulation

Why It Matters

On the first weekend of every month, 10-year-old Jon and his mother, Mia, visit Jon's grandparents, 2 hours away. After breakfast one Saturday morning, Mia tells Jon to feed the dog, get dressed, and bring his suitcase (which they packed the previous night) downstairs. Jon nods and smiles. He's excited about the trip. His intention is to follow his mother's instructions.

Mia goes upstairs to dress and 15 minutes later, she is ready to go. As she passes by Jon's room, she sees that his suitcase is still on his bed. She finds Jon in the yard—in his pajamas, playing with the dog. Mia is exasperated. "What is his problem? Yes, he has ADHD, but how hard is it to do three simple things? He loves to go to his grandparents' house! Why is it always such a struggle to get him to listen?"

In spite of Jon's commitment to following his mother's instructions, he has—once again—failed to bring his behavior in line with his intentions. Mia is at a loss to explain Jon's behavior, but she knows what her sister Lynn believes, because she has heard Lynn's opinion dozens of times: "Jon is just spoiled. He pays attention fine when he's playing video games or soccer. You need to be stricter!" Lynn thinks that Jon's failure to comply is due to a lack of motivation–if he wanted to do it, he could. But Mia, a 30-year-old single mother, isn't so sure. She's been consistent with discipline. She works at a school, where she sees children who aren't disciplined at home, and she knows that Jon's problems are different than theirs. Mia also knows that Jon feels bad about himself when he doesn't succeed at school or when she constantly fusses at him at home. She knows that he has begun to compare himself to his peers and is frustrated with his inability to accomplish simple things that seem effortless for his friends. She has heard him refer to himself as "dumb." She sees that he is genuinely remorseful that he did not get ready for their trip. She can't understand why Jon doesn't comply with the instructions he receives from adults, but she doesn't think it's a lack of motivation. She knows in her heart that he would comply if he could. She wishes she could somehow peer inside his mind and understand what is happening there.

Studying Self-Regulation

In the late 1960s, Walter Mischel and a team of researchers at Stanford University conducted a series of experiments that give us some insight into children's ability to bring their behavior in line with their intentions. The design of the experiment (called a delay of gratification paradigm) was simple: A researcher seated each child in turn at a table in a small, barren room and presented each one with a treat (their choice of a marshmallow, cookie, or pretzel). The researcher told the children that if they waited a little while to eat the treat, they could have two treats instead of just one. The researcher then left the room.

Almost all of the children wanted to have the two treats. In other words, almost all of the children intended to behave in a certain way—to delay immediate gratification and thus obtain a preferred, but longer-term, outcome. But when the researcher left the room and the children were alone, only some of them were able to actually regulate their behavior in a way that allowed them to achieve that outcome. The others, influenced by the enticing presence of the treat before them, behaved in a way that brought immediate pleasure—they ate the treat—but did not earn them their preferred two treats (Mischel, Shoda, & Rodriguez, 1989). Like Jon, they were not able to bring their behavior in line with their intentions.

The Space Between Stimulus and Response

One of the goals of the Stanford researchers was to identify the mental processes that allow people to delay gratification. By leaving the children alone in the room, they were able to observe how the children behaved during that space of time between the *stimulus* (the offer of either one treat or two) and the child's ultimate *response* (the act of eating the treat.) What were the differences in the ways children used that space of time?

The researchers, watching from another room, noted that the children who were unable to wait for the second treat (weak self-regulators) often stared straight at the treat. In contrast, the children who were able to wait (strong self-regulators) often covered their eyes to avoid looking at the treat or distracted themselves with other activities such as singing a song or inventing games to play with their hands and feet (Mischel et al., 1989). It appeared that the strong self-regulators had somehow acquired mental strategies that allowed them to bring their behavior in line with their intentions while the other children had no such strategies to help them delay their response. It is particularly noteworthy that the successful strategies were ones that the children directed toward themselves.

The setup of the experiment—children in the room with no adult present—removed many of the strategies that 4-year-olds might typically use to get what they want. We can easily imagine a 4-year-old at home begging for a shorter wait time, bargaining for better terms ("If I wait, can I have three treats instead of two?"), whining, throwing a tantrum, or sneaking a treat behind the parent's back. All of these methods would be directed *outward* toward other people or the environment. In the Stanford study, the strategy that the successful children used was to turn *inward:* during that space between stimulus and response, they utilized strategies that enabled them to consciously regulate their own thoughts, emotions, and behavior.

The Point of Performance

When psychologist Russell Barkley (1997) refers to that space between stimulus and response, he calls it "the point of performance." It is that particular time and place where we are called upon to recognize our options and commit ourselves to a course of action. It is a window of opportunity that is available only for a limited time. According to Barkley, *response inhibition* is the key to keeping that window of opportunity open long enough to consider our options and choose our path. Barkley cites response inhibition as the most fundamental of the brain's *executive functions* and the gateway to accessing the other executive functions such as *working memory, cognitive flexibility, planning,* and *problem solving* (Barkley, 1997). Applying Barkley's theory to the Stanford 4-year-olds, those who were able to inhibit their first response kept that window of opportunity open and were then able to access those other functions: they used their working memory to remind themselves that waiting would bring larger rewards; they shifted their attention temporarily in order to regulate their emotions; and they created a plan to help them cope with the waiting period. For those who acted more impulsively, despite their intentions, that window of opportunity closed.

Is it possible to help the impulsive children recognize that they have the power to regulate their response at the point of performance? Can we say to the child who went for the immediate treat: "Next time, would you like to be able to wait and get two treats? You would? Well, I can show you how!" The Stanford researchers, in a follow-up study, did just that. They taught the children various strategies, including how to use their thoughts as mental tools with which to regulate their attention and modulate their emotions and level of arousal. The impulsive children who were taught these mental strategies were indeed able to do a much better job of regulating their responses the next time around, performing as well as the children who were naturally strong inhibitors (Mischel et al., 1989). At least for that particular task, and that particular point of performance, the mental tricks that they had learned to utilize in that space between stimulus and response produced a more level playing field for the naturally impulsive children.

Executive Function

In recent years there has been a surge of interest in the concept of executive function. Barkley (1997) describes executive function as self-directed mental strategies that (1) occur during a delay in responding to an event; (2) serve to modify the eventual response; and (3) improve the future consequences related to the event. Barkley and others have posed theories that explain how these mental processes organize and order our behavior, allowing us to direct our actions through time toward a goal. Executive functions involve mental processes such as:

- Working memory: holding several pieces of information in mind while we try to do something with them—for example, understand and solve a problem or carry out a task.
- Response inhibition: inhibiting actions that interfere with our intentions or goals.
- Shifting focus: interrupting an ongoing response in order to direct attention to other aspects of a situation that are important for goal attainment.
- Cognitive flexibility: generating alternative methods of solving a problem or reaching a goal.
- Self-monitoring: checking on one's own cognitions and actions to ensure that they are in line with one's intentions.
- Goal orientation: creating and carrying out a multistep plan for achieving a goal in a timely fashion, keeping the big picture in mind.

For an example of how executive functions allow intentional, goal-directed behavior, let's return to Jon and Mia. On the evening before their trip to Jon's grandparents, Mia arrives at home after work. She has 2 hours alone at home before she'll need to pick Jon up from his friend's house.

Mia picks up the mail and sorts through it. Her favorite magazine is in the stack, and she feels a deep sense of relaxation as she pictures herself sinking into her recliner and reading it. But as she heads toward the chair, she recalls (working memory) that she needs to make a cake for her mother's birthday. She wants to get the cake baked before she picks Jon up from his friend's house after soccer practice (goal orientation). She reluctantly leaves the magazine on the recliner for later (shifting focus), goes to the kitchen, and gets out the recipe. Still finding herself thinking about how much time baking the cake entails and feeling reluctant to get started (self-monitoring), she reminds herself how pleased her mother will be with the cake—an old family recipe (shifting focus, cognitive flexibility). She recalls that she was 8 years old when she first baked the cake, with her mother's help. She begins to feel more energized. As she gathers the ingredients, her phone rings. She checks the display and decides not to answer (response inhibition). She tells herself that she can return her friend's call after the cake is in the oven (cognitive flexibility, goal orientation). While working, Mia recalls (working memory) a TV show she had planned to watch. She checks the clock and sees that it is time for the show to start. She makes a decision not to watch it (response inhibition). If she ends up with free time, she would rather use it talking with her friend (goal orientation). She slips the cake into the oven, sets the timer, glances at the clock (self-monitoring), and notes that when the cake is ready it will be time to leave to pick up Jon (goal orientation). She decides to clean the kitchen so she can relax and enjoy the rest of the evening (goal orientation). She loads the dishwasher, turns it on, and then sits down in her recliner—putting her magazine aside—and returns her friend's call (working memory, shifting focus). The two friends talk until the timer rings. Then Mia takes out the cake, remembers to turn off the oven (working memory), grabs her purse, and goes to pick up Jon. She feels pleased and satisfied and is looking forward to spending the evening with Jon and visiting her parents tomorrow.

In the above example, Mia sets certain goals for herself: She wants to prepare a special cake for her mother's birthday, clean up the mess when finished, be on time to pick up her son, and—if possible—chat with her friend on the phone. Mia is able to regulate her thoughts and emotions and to successfully bring her behavior in line with her intentions. Mia takes this functioning for granted, but not every adult is blessed with the ability to execute multiple goals so smoothly and efficiently. Mia brings numerous assets to each situation she encounters: intelligence, talent, and good intentions. But if those assets were not combined with good executive functions, the outcome of Mia's evening might have been very different. The cake might have been only half started. She might have been late picking up Jon, upsetting him and inconveniencing his friend's family. She and Jon might have come home to a kitchen full of dirty dishes. Mia might have ended up feeling stressed and guilty rather than pleased and satisfied.

Delays in Development of Executive Function

Children differ greatly in their development of executive functions. At a given age, some children will have mastered the self-regulation tasks typical for that age group, while for others self-regulation is still emerging. Executive function is often delayed in children with specific disorders such as attention-deficit/hyperactivity disorder (ADHD), learning disabilities, and autism. For an example of delayed executive function in childhood, let's look at Jon, who has been diagnosed with ADHD.

Immediately after receiving his mother's instructions on Saturday morning, Jon gets the dog food and puts it in the dog's bowl. But when the dog brings him a ball, Jon responds to that stimulus and takes the ball. When the dog barks to go outside, Jon responds to that stimulus, and the boy and the dog enjoy a game of fetch in the yard. It is not until his mother opens the back door and steps into the yard, dressed for their trip, that Jon recalls that to be ready for the trip to see his grandparents, he was also supposed to get dressed and bring his suitcase downstairs.

In spite of Jon's good intentions, he fails to comply with his mother's instructions. Most children Jon's age would have little trouble remembering what needs to be done and ordering their actions toward completion of those few simple tasks. But like the impulsive preschoolers in the Stanford study, Jon has difficulty regulating his behavior to line up with his intentions. Because of delays in the development of his executive functions, his responses are often at the mercy of whatever stimulus most immediately captures his attention. Mia's instructions are stored in his memory—he knows what he is supposed to do. He retrieves the first task and acts on it: He feeds the dog. But his executive functioning is not strong enough for him to hold all of her instructions in mind (working memory) in a way that allows him to retrieve the other tasks and at the same time ignore competing stimuli such as the dog's desire to go outside and play ball (response inhibition). Like the 4-year-olds who ate the treat, Jon enjoys the sensations of the moment. He doesn't reflect (self-monitoring) on his actions until–at the sight of his mother–he recalls his initial intention of following her instructions. But as remorseful as he is about his failure to comply, the pattern of poor self-regulation is likely to repeat itself the next time he is given a set of instructions to follow. He has not acquired the mental strategies that Barkley describes as "actions we perform to ourselves and direct at ourselves so as to accomplish self-control, goal-directed behavior, and the maximization of future outcomes" (1997, p. 57).

Won't or Can't?

Unfortunately, deficits in executive function may appear to an onlooker to be a matter of laziness or lack of motivation. Many adults–such as Mia's sister Lynn–scoff at the idea that a child is developmentally unable to regulate his behavior and point to his ability to pay attention in certain activities, such as playing a video game or participating in a soccer match, as proof that the child "can pay attention when he wants to." However, what Lynn calls "paying attention" is really a reference to the operation of Jon's working memory. Following a series of instructions when he is alone–and has to rely on internally represented information–places a very different set of demands on Jon's working memory than does a video game or soccer match. The latter activities provide immediate and ongoing external cues and feedback at the point of performance that help him to direct his behavior. For example, in a soccer game, Jon is an attentive player, responding to directions from his coach, shouts from his teammates, and the immediate, physical, and ever-changing set of circumstances on the field. The rich social context of the game is constantly providing him with verbal and nonverbal cues that activate his working memory and enable him to initiate the right action at the right time, drawing on his considerable knowledge and skills. In short, the soccer game itself provides him with the external support he needs to regulate his behavior and perform in keeping with expectations.

In contrast, after Mia gives Jon instructions to get ready for their Saturday morning trip, she leaves the room. Once she is gone, there are no external cues or feedback, nothing to keep Jon on track but his own mental processes. For Jon to follow Mia's instructions in a timely manner, he must translate them into internally represented information. Recall that on Friday afternoon, Mia did this: strong working memory allows her to activate and focus on various pieces of stored information, manipulate those bits of data, and decide which ones to act on and when. The child with immature executive function is unable to do this. Because Jon's internal cueing and feedback system is weak, he ends up responding to cues from the environment instead. Barkley has stated that ADHD should be considered a "disorder of performance" (1997, p. 314), and Jon's actions on Saturday morning exemplify this: He knows what he needs to do and he has the skills to do it, but without significant external cues and feedback to compensate for his weak self-regulation, he cannot perform in keeping with his knowledge and skills.

External Support at the Point of Performance

One way to compensate for a lack of internal regulation is to use tools that externalize the executive functions. A simple example of a way to externalize an executive function is the time-honored habit of making a to-do list. If Mia sets aside an afternoon to run errands, she may decide first to make a list of things she needs to do. She could just rely on her working memory and hope that she remembers everything. But the list is a helpful tool; it gives external support to her working memory.

To be most effective, this external support should be available at the *point of performance* (Barkley, 1997). Making a list can be helpful in and of itself, as a way for Mia to organize her thoughts and make a plan. But it will be a far more helpful tool if she doesn't leave it at home. If she has it with her in a purse or pocket, it will always be available at the point of performance—when and where she needs to remember what to do next.

Mia eventually speaks with the school counselor about Jon's difficulties and learns about executive functions. The counselor refers her to a therapist, telling Mia that the therapist can teach Jon some strategies that will give him external support for his weak executive functions.

> At his first visit with the therapist, Jon is given an assignment to be carried out on the weekend. Chores have always been a source of tension between Jon and Mia. Mia feels frustrated when she has to give Jon reminders each and every step of the way in order for him to complete his chores. Jon's assignment from the therapist is to make a list to supplement his working memory and free him from depen-

dence on his mother's reminders. To engage Jon's interest and sense of fun, the therapist has given this tool a playful spin: It will be a "wrist list."

On Saturday, Jon sits down at the table and cuts a piece of paper into strips. He then writes his chores on the strips— one chore per strip. Next, with Mia's help, he puts them in the order that they are to be done. The final chore is his favorite—taking his dog to the park for a long walk. Finally, Jon puts the strips together to create a paper chain. Once the chain is completed, he attaches it to his wrist so that it will always be at the point of performance as he moves about the house completing his chores.

An hour later, chores done, Mia, Jon, and the dog are on their way to the park. "That was fun," Jon says to his mother. "And I got all my chores done by myself! Let's do that again next week."

In the above example, Jon uses a strategy that provides external support for his working memory. Although it does not necessarily improve through use of this strategy, he happily obtains his desired outcome. His mother is also happy with the outcome. She is pleased that the chores got done but is even more pleased to see that Jon himself is so satisfied. She sees that she was right: Jon is motivated to succeed. But she had been expecting him to succeed in ways that were not in line with his development. She now sees that, with the right kind of external support, Jon can experience the success that he wants so much for himself. Like the preschoolers who learned mental tricks to delay their response, Jon has learned that he can employ self-directed strategies to stay on track and act in accordance with his intentions.

An Experience of Empowerment:
Emphasizing the "Self" in Self-Regulation

Using these self-directed strategies to reach one's goals is a different experience than being directed by someone else, even if the same goals are reached. For example, on that Saturday morning when Jon failed to get ready for the trip to visit his grandparents, had Mia been there with him, reminding him of what he needed to do, he would have gladly complied. Even if Mia had just remained in the room with him, her presence would probably have been enough to cue Jon's working memory. We can also speculate that, if an adult had remained in the room with the 4-year-olds in the Stanford study, a larger percentage of the children would have been able to delay their response and wait for the larger reward. But it's one thing for a child to control his behavior in response to instructions or influence from others. It's a fundamentally different experience—and an empowering one—for a child to learn that by taking control of one's own mental resources, one can alter the outcome of an event. The children in the Stanford experiment who succeeded in acting on their intentions were strong self-regulators—they did not have to depend on others to regulate their behavior.

Common sense would lead us to hypothesize that the ability to regulate one's own behavior will have profound effects on one's quality of life. Research supports this. A long-term follow-up on the Stanford 4-year-olds showed that the children who were strong self-regulators developed into more cognitively and socially competent adolescents, achieving higher scholastic performance and coping better with frustration and stress (Mischel et al., 1989). Results from a similar long-term research project led by Terrie Moffitt and Avsholom Caspi have confirmed these findings: A young child's self-regulatory abilities are strong predictors of the child's future health, educational achievement, economic welfare, and criminal history. The 32-year study followed the children from birth to age 32, and the results were found to be independent of the child's IQ or social class (Moffitt et al., 2011).

Encouragingly, the same study also indicates that improvements to self-regulation during childhood lead to better adult outcomes (Moffitt et al., 2011). This research suggests that when we show children like Jon how to intentionally regulate their thoughts, emotions, and behavior, we can empower them to live a life in which they can act in accordance with their intentions, pursuing the goals and upholding the standards that are important to them. A publication by Harvard University's Center on the Developing Child (2011) reviews current research and concludes that the evidence base is strong enough to warrant putting much more effort into initiatives designed to deliberately cultivate self-regulation in children. We hope that this book makes some small contribution to that effort.

CHAPTER TWO

A Framework for Understanding Executive Function

FOR CHILDREN STRUGGLING WITH self-regulation, the terms and concepts of executive function (EF) can give them and their parents a new perspective on their problems. For example, when Jon and his mother learn about the concept of working memory, it helps them understand why Jon doesn't follow instructions, which leads them to adapt a practical strategy that Jon can use to improve his performance.

> After discussing Jon's failure to follow his mother's instructions to get ready for their trip, Jon's therapist tells him that his brain—just like everyone else's—has lots of different jobs. She asks Jon what kinds of jobs his brain is really good at. Jon is able to come up with a list: playing video games, making up songs, telling jokes, and figuring out how to score goals in soccer.
>
> The therapist explains that working memory is also one of the brain's jobs: "Our working memory helps us keep ideas in our minds so that we can take the right actions at the right time." The therapist engages Jon and his mother in playing a game in which he can demonstrate his working memory (Activity 2.1).

Activity 2.1.   Ready, Set, Go For It!

RATIONALE: Not everyone is blessed with a good working memory. It is important to know the limits of one's ability to work from memory. With that understanding, we can either (1) use practice to improve our working memory, or (2) find ways to give our memories a boost or a reminder by using memory helpers.

GOAL: This activity introduces the concept of working memory and gives the child an opportunity to test his or her working memory. It also helps the child to recognize the limits of working memory and to learn to use strategies to support memory.

MATERIALS NEEDED: Everyday objects.

EXPLANATION FOR CHILD: Sometimes we have to remember to do several things in a row. For example, when I go to the grocery store, I have to remember which things to get from the shelves. If there is just one thing to get, I don't need a grocery list. I just use my memory. But if I have to get a lot of things, my memory needs a helper. So I make a list. The list is a memory helper.

Let's play a game called **Ready, Set, Go for It!** Let's see how many things you can do from memory:

STEP 1: **READY =** I'll tell you what to do.
STEP 2: **SET =** You say back to me what you are supposed to do.
STEP 3: **GO FOR IT! =** That's your cue to go ahead and do it.
We'll start off easy and then get harder and harder. First, I'll give you just one thing to do. The next time I'll tell you two things. I will add one thing each time and we'll see how many things you can remember at once. When you get to where you have too many things to remember, we are going to use some memory helpers.

EXAMPLES:
Trial A: Bring me the *blue book* by the phone.
Trial B: Bring me the *red cup* by the sink and the *newspaper* from the coffee table.
Trial C: Bring me the *book sack* by the door, the *ruler* from the desk, and an *apple* from the bowl.

(continued)

Activity 2.1. Continued

USING MEMORY HELPERS:

When the child begins to have difficulty, teach the child to use memory helpers. Here's how: When you get to STEP 2 (**READY**), the child decides on a memory helper to give external support to his or her working memory. Some possibilities are:

Memory Helper #1: Before you say **Go for It!** have the child repeat the items aloud **three times** (instead of just once).

Memory Helper #2: Before you say **Go for it!** have the child make a list of the items. He can use words or draw quick pictures of the items.

Memory Helper #3: Encourage the child to come up with his or her own memory helpers.

After deciding on a memory helper, go on to STEP 3 (**GO FOR IT!**) Then discuss: Did the memory helper work? If not, try again, perhaps changing the memory helper to make it more effective.

SUGGESTIONS FOR EXPANDING THE ACTIVITY: This assignment helps the child understand the concept of working memory. Parent and child can also practice using working memory by continuing this activity at home. Keep it fun by practicing frequently, but for short periods of time.

VARIATION: Another game that involves working memory is **We're Going on a Trip.**

1. The first player says: We are going on a trip and we're taking _____ (Player names an item to bring on the trip.)
2. The next person says: We are going on a trip and we're taking _____ and _____. (Player has to say the item named by the first person and add another item.)
3. Keep it going: Each player has to recall all past items and add a new item. Continue until a player is unable to recall all items. Keep track as a group; count how many items were recalled before the game ended. Then play another round and try to do better each time. (It's okay to be silly with this game and throw in some wacky items!)

Adapted from **Simon Says Pay Attention** (Ready, Set, Go For It assignment), **p. 65, © Golden Path Games, 2009.**

The therapist points out that everyone's brain is different. Some people have strong working memories and it is easy for them to remember what they need to do. Other people find this really hard. The therapist tells Jon that her working memory isn't always perfect, so she often does things to help it out. She shows Jon some cue cards that she made to help her give a speech. Each cue card has a word and a picture, to remind her of all the things she wants to say. When she sees each cue, she remembers what to say next, just as Jon remembered what to do in response to the cues in the game that they played. The cue cards are a tool that she uses to help her working memory.

They review the jobs that Jon's brain is already good at. The therapist asks Jon if he would like to use a tool to help his working memory do a better job. He is eager to do so, and the therapist gives him an assignment to try the wrist list (see Chapter 1).

Although Jon had previously been diagnosed with ADHD, he did not have a clear understanding of what that meant. If asked, he would say, "I can't focus. I don't pay attention." He might add that he once took medicine to help him "focus better" but that it made him feel bad and he doesn't take it anymore. He has been told by his mother and teachers to try harder to pay attention to what he is doing, but he has not received any concrete explanation of what "paying attention" means or how to try harder at it.

We believe that the construct of executive function provides specific concepts and terminology that can help children learn that they themselves can do a great deal to improve their own performance. In this chapter, we (1) look at what the current research tells us about executive function, and

(2) translate that information into a child-friendly framework that clinicians can use to educate children and their families.

The Elusive Nature of Executive Function: Current Research

Interest in the study of executive function has increased dramatically in recent years. The scientific community has seen a number of new theories, a proliferation of studies, and many discussions and debates. There is no standardized definition of executive function. There is also a lack of agreement regarding its components and whether they are linked to a single underlying ability (the theory of unity) or are distinct yet related processes (the theory of diversity or separability). Furthermore, there is much debate about how to accurately measure components and functioning for both research and real-life applications. Perhaps the only belief that unites all of these viewpoints is that executive function is a very complex construct.

Defining Executive Function

A review of the literature produces a number of definitions of executive function:

- The ability to maintain an appropriate problem-solving set for the attainment of a future goal (Welsh & Pennington, 1988).
- Actions we perform to ourselves and direct at ourselves so as to accomplish self-control, goal-directed behavior, and the maximization of future outcomes (Barkley, 1997).
- Adaptive, goal-directed behaviors that enable individuals to override more automatic or established thoughts and responses (Garon, Bryson, & Smith, 2008).

- Abilities of goal formation, planning, carrying out goal-directed plans, and effective performance (Jurado & Roselli, 2007).
- A set of processes that all have to do with managing one-self and one's resources in order to achieve a goal. It is an umbrella term for neurologically based skills involving mental control and self-regulation (Cooper-Kahn & Dietzel, 2008).
- An umbrella term encompassing the goal-oriented functions of the prefrontal cortex, including ability to plan ahead, to reflect on performance, and to alter that performance if necessary (Best, Miller, & Jones, 2009).

Which Brain Functions Are Executive in Nature?

Researchers have yet to agree on what abilities are included in executive function. Lists offered by experts have included as many as 33 concepts (Barkley, 2011). Some of the executive functions cited in the literature aimed at the general public include activation, focus, effort, emotion, memory, and action (Brown, 2005); working memory, planning and prioritization, organization, time management, metacognition, response inhibition, emotional control, sustained attention, task initiation, goal-directed persistence, and flexibility (Dawson & Guare, 2009); inhibition, shift, emotional control, initiation, working memory, planning and organization, organization of materials, and self-monitoring (Cooper-Kahn & Dietzel, 2008).

The scientific literature focuses on a narrower list of functions. The Center on the Developing Child (2011) cited three dimensions of executive functioning that are most frequently highlighted by scientists: working memory, inhibitory control, and cognitive flexibility. Best and colleagues, in a 2009 review, cited the same three functions or components with some slight differences in conceptualization or terminology. For example, working memory is sometimes conceptualized as *updating*. Cognitive flexibility is often referred to as *shifting* or *set shifting*. Also, in addition to the three foundational functions, a fourth function, *planning*, is sometimes cited in the literature as critical to goal-oriented behavior.

Researchers studying executive function in the laboratory attempt to isolate each of its components as much as possible, in order to determine its unique developmental course, its mediation by the prefrontal cortex, its effects on behavior, and its correlation to other components. Other experts construct theories that correlate more closely with day-to-day functioning. As noted in Chapter 1, Russell Barkley, whose primary interest is in applying executive function theory to understanding ADHD, considers behavioral inhibition as the primordial executive function upon which the development of the other functions depends. He cites four other executive functions:

1. Nonverbal working memory: holding events in mind, sense of time, forethought, hindsight, and self-awareness
2. Internalized speech or verbal working memory: speech directed toward the self, self-questioning, self-directing, and generation of rules
3. Reconstitution: creativity and problem solving, playing with ideas and behaviors by taking them apart and reassembling them to form novel solutions
4. Self-regulation of affect, motivation, and arousal

Barkley (1997) states that, working together, these executive functions allow for behavioral control, which includes execution of goal-directed responses, goal-directed persistence, task reengagement following disruption, sensitivity to response feedback, and behavioral flexibility.

Neurological Basis of Executive Function

According to the Center on the Developing Child (2011), scientists are making strides in showing how these mental processes are mediated in the brain. Their review of the research indicates that while the prefrontal cortex is the primary brain region involved, the anterior cingulate, parietal cortex, and hippocampus also play a role. What we see in the child's behavior—the gradual improvement of executive functioning from infancy to late adolescence—corresponds closely with the physical development of these prefrontal brain regions, as circuits and systems emerge and forge connections. While relatively little is known about how specific developmental changes in the frontal cortex are related to specific changes in children's executive function, an increasing number of studies are addressing this topic (Zelazo & Paus, 2010).

A Child-Friendly Framework for Explaining Executive Function

In our clinical work with children and their families, we have used these concepts and theories as the basis for developing a practical framework for interpreting executive function–related difficulties to children and families. Our categories are similar to the core components most often identified by researchers (working memory or updating, response inhibition, and shifting or cognitive flexibility), but each of ours is also somewhat of a hybrid, combining concepts and behaviors to correspond more closely to the presenting problems that we typically see. We also borrow ideas from Barkley's theory as it offers functional explanations of how the various components impact day-to-day life.

Our four categories (each with its own child-friendly definition):

1. Working memory: remembering to do the right thing at the right time.
2. Response inhibition: stopping yourself from doing the wrong thing.
3. Shifting focus: making yourself stop thinking about one thing so you can start thinking about (and then doing) something else.
4. Goal orientation: making a good plan for what you are going to do and then following your plan and getting it done on time.

Working Memory

Working memory refers to the brain processes that are used to temporarily hold, organize, and manipulate information. The information is already stored in the brain; working memory is the process of activating and focusing on pieces of that stored information. Working memory enables us to hold several pieces of information in mind while we try to do something with them—for example, understand and solve a problem or carry out a task. Some researchers refer to working memory as updating, which reminds us of its fluid nature: We are constantly adding and deleting information from our working memory depending on changes in events or changes in our way of evaluating those events.

In its simplest form, working memory allows us to hold

information in mind in order to intentionally perform an action. For example, we see working memory in operation when an infant begins to intentionally make certain physical actions (for example, kicking a foot) in order to achieve a goal (making the crib mobile move). This action first occurs randomly, as the infant kicks its legs, hits the mobile overhead, and causes it to move. Over time, working memory allows the baby to make a connection between its own action and the movement of the mobile, to hold that information in mind, and eventually to learn to intentionally repeat the sequence of events.

As the child matures, he becomes capable of holding more than one piece of information in mind. Barkley (1997) separates working memory into two types: *nonverbal* and *verbal* working memory (which he refers to as *internalized language*). Our framework uses this verbal working memory, the one related to internalized, or self-directed, language. Researcher Akira Miyake has documented the significance of internalized language as a retrieval aid for task goals, acting as a "self-cuing" device (Miyake, Emerson, Padilla, & Ahn, 2004). It is, at least in part, our capacity for internalized language that enables us to hold multiple pieces of information in mind, manipulate them, and use them to direct our own behavior.

Laura Berk (1994) has studied self-directed language in children, particularly in early development when language has not yet been completely internalized and exists in a semi-overt form as "private speech"—speech that is spoken aloud but which is directed toward oneself. The fact that it is spoken out loud allows researchers to observe the content of this self-directed language, which is more difficult once language has become internalized. Berk notes that private speech is often regarded as a sign of inattentiveness or immaturity. In her research, however, Berk found that the central function of private speech is self-regulation. During observations in the classroom, she also noted that private speech increases with task difficulty, especially when the teacher is not available to provide assistance, an indication that private speech (and its subsequent form, internalized language) is a tool that helps us direct our actions more effectively (Berk, 1994).

Other researchers have found that specific kinds of self-directed language are important for task completion. For example, researchers have found that when children use an "if-then" or "when-then" formula to state their intention (rather than simply saying what their intention is), they are better able to perform desired behaviors and to inhibit unwanted behaviors while performing a task. One computer-based task required children to press a key when they saw a particular picture, but to refrain from pressing the key if the picture was accompanied by a sound. Some children were instructed to say to themselves, "I will not press a key for pictures that have a sound"—a simple, straightforward statement of intent. Other children were instructed to say to themselves, "If I hear a sound, then I will not press a key." This difference in their self-directed language made a big difference in their subsequent actions. The children who used the if-then formulation performed significantly better than those who used a simple statement of their intention (Gawrilow, Gollwitzer, & Oettingen, 2011).

The if-then formula appears to have provided the children with specific, self-directed instructions that they were able to hold in their working memory and use at the point of performance: that space between stimulus (hearing the sound) and response (refraining from pressing the key). We can hypothesize from this that self-directed language is an integral part of working memory and that the more effective one's self-directed language is, the better one will be able to hold information in mind and covertly hold a dialogue with oneself –observing, questioning, monitoring, and guiding one's actions. In our example in Chapter 1, Mia's working memory provides a way for her to temporarily store, organize, and manipulate information as she decides what actions to perform (and which to inhibit). She activates information that is already stored in her brain and holds a sort of inner dialogue with herself, deciding which bits of information she needs to act on. She focuses her attention on one task as she executes it, while holding the other tasks in line for their turn. Because of the mature functioning of her working memory or internalized language, Mia is not at the mercy of her environment: instead of responding only to external stimuli, she is able to use language to generate her own internal stimuli. In contrast, her son Jon responds more readily to external stimuli than to internally generated stimuli.

Response Inhibition

Response inhibition refers to one's ability to refrain from doing things that do not contribute to one's intentions or goals. Many researchers believe that working memory and behavioral inhibition have a close, reciprocal relationship (Garon et al., 2008). In the previous section, we gave an example of how working memory allows an infant to hold information in mind in order to intentionally make an action that causes an effect (kicking a foot to make the crib mobile move). While doing so, the infant also has to inhibit other movements that do not lead to the desired effect.

When the infant inhibits random movements in order to make intentional movements, the response inhibition has an immediate benefit of allowing the activation of the intended action. As the child matures, however, he must also inhibit behaviors for their long-term benefits. For example, hitting a friend might produce the immediate benefit of stopping the friend from taking a toy, but the child is expected to inhibit this response, forgo that immediate benefit, and enjoy the longer-term benefit that comes from pausing and then using other means of negotiation. An older school-age child needs to inhibit any number of behaviors that have longer-range consequences: for example, the urge to daydream during class or to watch TV instead of doing homework.

Barkley proposes that response inhibition is really three interrelated processes:

1. The ability to refrain from executing one's natural (prepotent) response to a situation
2. The ability to perform "interference control" once a course of action has been initiated, and thus protect the response from disruption by competing events and responses
3. The ability to interrupt a response once it has been initiated (Barkley, 1997)

Inhibiting the Prepotent Response

The prepotent response is one's immediate and natural response to a stimulus. Response inhibition does not refer only to behavior; it can also refer to inhibiting one's automatic perception or thought about what happens.

The ability to suppress one's natural, immediate response

to a stimulus provides the opportunity to choose alternative responses. When one fails to inhibit the prepotent response, that opportunity may be lost and other alternatives may no longer be available. In the Stanford study cited in Chapter 1 (Mischel et al., 1989), the natural, prepotent response for 4-year-olds would be to eat the treat that is placed in front of them. Some of the children grabbed the treat right away, without even considering the option of waiting. They achieved immediate gratification but the opportunity to earn two treats was gone. Those who paused had the opportunity to earn a second treat.

Interference Control

Inhibiting the prepotent response may be only the beginning of the self-control needed to achieve a desired long-term outcome. Once that pause behavior is initiated, the individual needs to resist competing behaviors and filter out distractions in order to stay on track toward the goal.

It was the difficulty of resisting competing behaviors that was the downfall of the 4-year-olds who intended, but were unable, to wait and get the second treat. To be successful, they had to continue to pause under very challenging circumstances: an enticing treat right in front of them and no adult in the room. The children who were strong self-regulators had strategies that they could direct toward themselves—thinking of something else, reminding themselves of their goal—that appeared to help them protect that pause. The children without successful strategies for protecting the pause were unable to continue to inhibit the prepotent response, and therefore did not obtain their preferred outcome.

In our example in Chapter 1, in order to stay on track with

her intentions Mia inhibits a number of prepotent responses. For example, while she is mixing the cake, her phone rings: she inhibits the response of answering the call to finish preparing the cake. A little later, she recalls that it is time for a favorite TV program, but inhibits any thoughts about watching it, because she wants to return her friend's call. Her son Jon has much more difficulty filtering out distractions. When he receives instructions and performs the first task (feeding the dog), he simultaneously inhibits any competing prepotent responses—such as dawdling at the table or wandering off and watching TV. However, he is unable to continue to inhibit competing responses. When his dog presents other stimuli (bringing him a ball and barking to go outside), he responds to those. Jon lacks the internal capacity for performing interference control.

We discuss Barkley's third type of response inhibition—stopping an ongoing response—in the next section.

Shifting Focus

We have addressed the importance of working memory and response inhibition. Both of these functions enable us to stay on track in relation to our intention or goal. However, it is equally important sometimes to be able to get off track, to shift focus in response to changing situations or new information. As we use the term in this book, shifting focus refers to a multistep process, a combination of several executive function components: first, self-monitoring (working memory to determine if an ongoing response is in one's best interest); second, interruption of an ongoing response if it is not in line with one's intentions; and third, cognitive flexibility (considering alternative ways of perceiving or behaving).

Self-Monitoring

As noted previously, another term for working memory is updating, signifying the fluid nature of working memory in response to the unfolding of events. This fluid nature of working memory allows us to self-monitor—to reflect on our initial response to an event and on the likely consequences of that response.

In our example in Chapter 1, when Mia returns home on Friday afternoon she recognizes that she has conflicting intentions for the use of her 2 hours of time. One intention—which she has already begun to act on—is to sit and read and relax. A previous intention—which she has just recalled—is to bake a cake for her mother's birthday. The executive function of working memory or updating allows her to reflect on both of these intentions simultaneously.

Interrupting the Ongoing Response

Once Mia recognizes that her current response is not in line with her intentions, she must interrupt it. Mia stops herself from sitting in the chair and leaves the magazine there for later.

Cognitive Flexibility

We had noted previously that working memory enables an individual to hold multiple pieces of information in mind for the purpose of goal completion. Cognitive flexibility enables us to manipulate that information, weighing multiple options for the resolution of a problem, considering different perspectives (including the perspectives of others), and comparing past consequences and possible future outcomes. Barkley

(1997) refers to cognitive flexibility as reconstitution, the covert analysis and synthesis of behavior. He states that this executive function allows us to mentally play with ideas or behaviors, rehearsing our responses before we implement them. Various combinations of behaviors can be covertly constructed and tested out before one is eventually selected for performance.

After Mia goes to the kitchen and gets out the recipe, she finds herself reluctant to get started, still tempted to just sit and relax. She then recalls memories about the recipe and thinks about how pleased her mother will be tomorrow. As she covertly plays with this information and mentally rehearses different options, she also covertly experiences the emotional ramifications of the various options. This allows her to regulate her emotions in the current moment: her feeling of reluctance fades and she feels more energized and committed to her plan.

In this example, Mia's ability to think flexibly about her situation brings about a corresponding change in her emotional and motivational state, which in turn makes it easier for her to stay on track toward her goal. In the Stanford study, the 4-year-olds who were strong self-regulators seemed to have the capacity for cognitive flexibility—and it appeared to affect their level of arousal and their emotions. They were able to flexibly shift their attention away from the enticing properties of the treat and toward other thoughts and activities; this presumably helped them to remain calm and reach their intended goal. The weak self-regulators, on the other hand, appeared to be much less flexible in their responses: They often stared straight at the treat, and we can guess that their thoughts were primarily about its enticing qualities.

This presumably kept them in an aroused emotional state and made it difficult to wait and reach their intended goal. The researchers later taught the impulsive children mental strategies to help them protect the period of delay. These mental tricks were ways to think differently about the stimulus—for example, one of the tricks was to think of the marshmallow as a fluffy cloud, or the pretzels as little brown logs. Another trick was to think about the arousing qualities of a different treat—the children who had selected marshmallows were instructed to think about the taste of salty, crunchy pretzels. The researchers essentially gave the children a way to achieve some cognitive flexibility. And it worked: armed with those strategies, the impulsive children were able to protect their period of delay much longer (Mischel et al., 1989).

The researchers observed behaviors indicating that the strong self-regulators, even when they were distracting themselves by playing or singing a song, were simultaneously able to keep their longer-term goal in mind. For example, sometimes the children stopped their distracting play and seemed on the verge of eating the treat, but then verbally reminded themselves of the contingency (that waiting would earn them two treats) and returned to their distracting play (Mischel et al., 1989). The children were able to shift back and forth between these two mental processes, each supporting their intentions in different ways.

Goal Orientation

The final component in our executive function framework is goal orientation (which includes what some researchers label *planning* and what Barkley calls *nonverbal working memory*). It refers to the ability to make a plan for achieving a goal, and then to hold that information in mind as one activates and executes all aspects of that plan. It also includes a sense of time and an ability to motivate oneself and monitor one's progress through time toward a goal. Essentially, goal orientation means having an internal guide that allows for purposeful, goal-directed, and timely behavior.

Within the construct of goal orientation, the other executive functions—working memory, response inhibition, cognitive flexibility—operate smoothly. Working memory and cognitive flexibility allow for the creation of a plan: The individual covertly rehearses possibilities and selects the best actions for achieving a goal. Cognitive flexibility also fosters the motivation or drive necessary to initiate and maintain these actions. According to Barkley (1997), working memory and interference control, then serve to drive the plan toward its intended destination (creating goal-directed persistence); at the same time working memory provides continuous feedback (self-monitoring), thereby creating a sensitivity to errors and continued cognitive and behavioral flexibility.

Externalizing Executive Functions

In the above example, Mia's process of goal orientation all takes place internally. When her 10-year-old son Jon visits the therapist, he learns a strategy (using a wrist list for his Saturday morning chores) that externalizes the process of goal orientation (Table 2.1).

On the outside, Jon's process of goal orientation looks very different from Mia's. Mia's process is internalized and hidden from view. Jon's process is externalized, observable. But in both cases, not only did they accomplish their goals, but

TABLE 2.1. Internalized and Externalized Goal Orientation

Mia: Internalized Goal Orientation	Jon: Externalized Goal Orientation
Mentally reviews a list of the tasks that she wants to accomplish.	Creates an external representation of the tasks he needs to accomplish by writing each one on a slip of paper.
Mentally prioritizes and decides on the order for performing the various tasks.	Orders the tasks by physically arranging the slips of paper and linking them into a paper chain.
Relies on internalized language to remind herself of her goal and motivate herself.	Attaches the paper chain to his wrist to remind himself of his goal and motivate himself.
Relies on her working memory and cognitive flexibility to complete each task in turn and to monitor her progress.	Stays on track by removing one link at a time and performing that task. The dwindling chain of links provides him with a visual indication of the progress he is making toward completion of his goals.

their strategies were self-directed. That, in the final analysis, is the essence of executive function: self-directed strategies for accomplishing one's intentions and goals. The process of creating and using the wrist list allowed Jon to achieve that all-important self-regulation: He no longer had to rely on his mother's reminders and prompting to complete his chores.

According to Barkley, both the internalized and externalized forms of behavior achieve self-regulation "and so are 'executive' in nature" (1997, p. 58).

Jon's success in using an externalized form of executive function demonstrates that children can learn strategies that will help them to become more self-directed. In the next chapter, we continue Jon's story along with the stories of three other children who struggle with self-regulation. These stories will demonstrate their need for greater external support for their executive functions.

CHAPTER THREE

Executive Function in the Everyday Lives of Children

AS NOTED IN CHAPTER 1, it is one thing for a child to control his or her behavior in response to instructions or influence from others. But it's a very different experience for a child to learn that by taking control of one's own mental resources one can alter the outcome of an event. Mature executive functioning means that the child can make use of self-directed strategies to act in accordance with his or her own values, intentions, and goals.

In Chapters 1 and 2, we introduced 10-year-old Jon, who has difficulty regulating his actions when he is on his own. In this chapter, we take a closer look at some day-to-day challenges for Jon and for three other children who struggle with self-regulation. We compare each child's behaviors with those of a child whose executive functioning is more mature. In these examples, we note an observation that we hear over and over from the parents of these children: The usual methods of discipline—a system of rewards and punishments or positive and negative consequences—do not seem to have any effect on the poor self-regulation shown by these children. On the other hand, we will see how the parents—and other concerned persons—intuitively provide external support for these children, helping them to compensate for their executive function weaknesses.

Each case example highlights one of the four components outlined in Chapter 2. Note, however, that because the functions are closely related, difficulty in one function is often an indication of difficulty in others as well.

1. Jon (age 10): working memory/internalized language
2. Connor (age 9): response inhibition
3. Amanda (age 4): shifting focus
4. Marcus (age 7): goal orientation

Jon: Working Memory

Over the years, Mia has learned to be very structured in the morning routine for her son Jon. Their next door neighbor and Jon's best friend, Pierre, is in Jon's class at school, and the boys ride the bus together. On school days, Pierre walks over to Jon's house at 7:00 A.M. and the boys walk together to the corner to meet the bus.

> On this morning at 5:55 A.M., Jon wakes up to an alarm clock (which Mia set the night before). Jon gets out of bed easily and goes downstairs for breakfast. He asks, as he often does, if he can watch TV. Mia replies, as she has for the past 6 months, that he can watch TV if he is completely ready for school.

Eliminating TV is one way Mia has structured their morning routine. Previously, Jon watched TV while he ate breakfast, and his breakfast would often last an hour. Six months ago Mia told Jon that he could watch TV on school days only after he completed what was required of him. She thought that would motivate Jon to get ready for school in a more timely fashion. However, after the first few days, it made no difference. This lack of response to consequences is a pattern that Mia has noted over the years. She takes privileges away—as she did with the TV—and though Jon may express disappointment initially, he does not seem motivated to earn the privilege back. She knows that he would like to watch TV in the morning, but if she doesn't allow it, in the end he seems perfectly content without it. In a similar way, when he was younger and she put him in time out as a consequence, he always seemed perfectly happy. He would play with whatever he had on hand—his shoelaces or a button or piece of string—until his time out was complete. And the time out never seemed to have much influence on his future behavior.

> Jon and Mia talk as she prepares their breakfast and as they eat together. At 6:20 Mia finishes her meal and puts her dishes in the dishwasher, but Jon is still eating. She is reluctant to leave him, knowing from experience that he can sit there for 30 minutes with a bowl of cereal. Before leaving the kitchen, Mia sets a timer for 5 minutes. She tells Jon that when the timer rings he has to go upstairs and get dressed. She also reminds him to put his dishes in the dishwasher. She then goes to her room to get ready for work. When the timer rings, Jon gets up and goes upstairs to get dressed, leaving his dishes on the table.

Mia can't rely on Jon to remember to move on to the next step in the morning routine. She sets the timer as a reminder. Jon complies with one of her two instructions. He is an easygoing child who likes to please his mother; his lack of cooperation is not due to defiance of any kind. But unless Mia is present or he has some other cue, like the timer, he often fails to initiate the next task. Although their new morning routine has been in place for 6 months, it has not become internalized. As Mia sometimes says, "It's as if every day it is all new to him, as if he has never done this before." His working memory needs extensive support for him to be able to initiate the series of actions that he needs to take to be ready for school.

Another thing that is noteworthy in their morning routine is that Jon loves to talk. If Mia would stay downstairs with him, he would talk and eat for an hour. As a toddler, he spoke early, and he has always been a big talker. When he was younger, "talking out of turn" was the most frequent complaint his teachers had about him. They reported that his primary interest at school seemed to be engaging in conversation with the children around him.

As discussed in Chapter 2, Barkley (1997) equates verbal working memory with internalized language, or using language to direct one's own behavior. One explanation for Jon's poor working memory is that, despite his language skills in conversation (externally directed language), Jon does not use language as well internally; he may not be using it effectively to direct his own behavior.

In Jon's room, his clothes for the day are neatly folded on a chair, placed there by Mia the night before. Jon begins to get dressed but then sits to look at the fish in his aquarium. At 6:40 his mother comes by his room and fusses at him, telling him to hurry up, that Pierre will be there soon.

We don't know what is going on in Jon's mind as he gazes at the fish (once he said he was wondering what it would be like to be a fish), but he is probably not reminding himself that he needs to get going so he can watch TV or be ready when Pierre arrives. Jon is not using language to direct himself toward his 7:00 A.M. departure time. The clothes laid out for him act as a cue that he needs to get dressed, but after beginning that task, he doesn't stay on track. His thoughts go elsewhere and his actions follow his thoughts.

Next door, Jon's friend Pierre has a more difficult time waking up, but once awake, he is able to keep in mind all of the things that he needs to do, and to do the right thing at the right time.

> Pierre's mother wakes him up at 6:00 A.M. As usual, he doesn't wake up easily, so it is not until his stepfather calls him another two times that he actually gets out of bed at 6:10. He comes downstairs where his mother has prepared breakfast. They talk together as he eats a waffle and an egg. At 6:20, he says, "I gotta go" and goes back upstairs. He dresses for school, brushes his teeth, combs his hair, and makes his bed. As he heads downstairs at 6:35, he calls out to his mother, who is dressing in her room, "I'm ready for school. I'm going downstairs," without pausing for an answer.

Pierre's stepfather works from home and Pierre likes to spend time with him in the morning before school. When Pierre was in second grade his mother made a rule: He could hang out with his stepfather only after he was completely ready for school. This had an immediate effect on Pierre's behavior in the morning. He became more independent and got ready quickly in order to have more time to spend with his stepfather.

> Pierre goes downstairs where his stepfather is watching the news while folding clothes. He helps his stepfather and they talk about the news and joke and laugh as they work. Pierre recalls that he needs to get a permission slip signed, gets it from his book sack, and has his stepfather sign it. He puts his book sack by the door and returns to folding clothes and talking. At 6:45, Pierre's stepfather takes the folded clothes upstairs. Pierre goes to the computer and begins playing a game. At 6:55 Pierre glances at the clock and says to himself, "Time to go." He leaves the computer and calls upstairs, "I'm leaving. See you this afternoon." His mother comes down and gives him a hug as he puts on his jacket and picks up his book sack. He heads next door to Jon's house.

In its simplest form, working memory is the ability to hold pieces of information in mind for the purpose of completing a task. Working memory allows our actions to be self-directed and frees us from being unduly influenced by immediate circumstances and contingencies. Pierre is able to hold in mind all of the actions that he needs to take in order to be ready for school: eat breakfast, dress, brush teeth, comb hair, make bed, and so on. Other than being woken by his parents, he does not require external reminders of what he needs to do. He is able to internally direct his actions. Even with distractions (talking to his mother and later his stepfather, watching the news, playing on the computer), he is still holding in mind the things he needs to do, and it is that internal information, rather than the external influences, that directs his behavior.

Like Jon, Pierre uses language to converse with others, but we can also see evidence of Pierre using it to guide his behavior. For example, after eating his breakfast, he says, "I gotta go." After he has finished dressing, he calls out, "I'm ready for school. I'm going downstairs." When he is on the computer, he glances at the clock and says, "I gotta go." He is directing and monitoring himself with language as he moves from one step in his routine to the next. It is likely that he is also covertly using language in his mind to guide himself during many other steps of his routine.

Next door, Jon also comes downstairs, but he needs more external reminders to complete his morning routine.

> Jon meets Mia downstairs at 6:45. She sends him back upstairs to comb his hair and brush his teeth. At 6:55 she calls up to him to hurry or he'll miss the bus. He comes downstairs at 6:59. She hands him his jacket and book sack and sends him out the door just as Pierre walks up.
>
> A minute later he comes back in; Pierre had reminded him about the permission slip that needed to be signed. Mia signs the paper, complaining that she does not have time to look at what she is signing. Jon runs out the door, joining Pierre at the bus stop. Mia shakes her head as she watches the boys run off.

Mia is grateful for Pierre's friendship with Jon. Pierre seems to intuitively understand Jon's difficulties, and he makes a point of helping Jon remember the things he needs to do (Table 3.1). Pierre isn't the only one who helps Jon out. Jon's sense of humor and kindheartedness earn him friends wherever he goes. His teachers and his coaches are patient with him, giving him reminders and second chances that they

TABLE 3.1. Comparison of Pierre and Jon's Working Memory and Internalized Language

	Pierre	Jon
Task: Remembering to do the right thing at the right time	Initiates routine actions (e.g., eat, get dressed, brush teeth, comb hair) at the right time based on internalized information.	More often than not does not initiate the routine actions at the right time; does not appear to be guided by internalized information.
	Recalls need to initiate nonroutine actions (get permission slip signed).	Does not recall need to initiate nonroutine actions (get permission slip signed).
	Appears to use language ("I'm ready now. I'm going downstairs." "Time to go." "I'm leaving.") to motivate and keep himself on track.	Does not appear to use language to either motivate himself or direct his actions.
Response to consequences	Three years ago, in second grade, became more independent and reliable about getting ready in the morning, motivated by the positive consequence of spending more time with his stepfather.	Consequence set up by mother (he can watch TV only after he is ready for school) has not motivated him to be more independent and reliable about getting ready in the morning.

might not extend to other children. But Mia is beginning to feel deeply concerned about Jon's future. She doesn't tell anyone, but she worries that he will turn out like his father. She met Jon's father when they were both in high school and, like Jon, he was easygoing, charming, and likeable. But he did not turn out to be a reliable husband or father and now is not a regular part of Jon's life. He lives in another state, pays child support erratically, and is currently unemployed. He makes promises to Jon and does not follow through. Mia loves her son deeply, and she doesn't want him to turn out to be the kind of man, or the kind of father, that his own father is.

She feels a sense of relief now that they have met with the therapist. Jon's pleasure in completing his chores on his own confirmed Mia's belief that Jon very much wants to succeed. She is now hopeful that she can find a way to help him and she looks forward to their next visit with the therapist.

Connor: Response Inhibition

Jason is taking his son, Connor, on an overnight campout with several other boys from Connor's Scout troop. They travel by car with another father, Gil, and his two sons, Paul (age 8) and Owen (age 5). They join three other fathers along with their boys, for a total of eight boys. All of the boys know each other from Scouts and from school. Connor is the oldest at age 9; there are four 8-year-olds, one 7-year-old, and two little brothers, both age 5. This is Connor's first camping trip and both Connor and Jason are looking forward to it.

Jason, Connor, and their traveling companions arrive at Camp Wildwood at 2:00 P.M. The other members of their group are already there and are assembling their tents. Jason and Connor bring their tent to the campsite. Jason tells Connor to begin taking the tent out of its bag, while he gets the other gear from the car. When he returns, the tent is untouched and Connor is down by the lake. Jason notices that all of the other boys, even the 5-year-olds, are working on their tents. He calls Connor back to the campsite and engages him in unpacking and assembling the tent.

Response inhibition includes the ability to refrain from executing one's natural (prepotent) response to a situation. Certainly, for a young boy, a natural response to the presence of a lake would be to run down to it. Jason sympathizes with Connor's behavior. Although all of the other boys have refrained from running down to the lake, he attributes the difference to this being Connor's first camping trip and also reflects that perhaps he shouldn't have left Connor by himself while he went back to the car.

Once the tents are set up, Rob, the organizer of the trip, assigns various chores to the older boys. Connor and Paul are instructed to pick up wood for the campfire and stack it near the cookout area. Connor and Paul go to the edge of the woods and begin picking up sticks and logs and bringing them to the campsite, devising an informal contest to see who can carry the most in one load. After several trips, they have a huge pile. When they start to head back to the woods, Rob reminds them to sort and stack the wood. Paul stops and begins to sort the branches from the larger logs, creating several stacks.

Connor says, "That's boring," and tries to convince Paul to continue gathering wood. When Paul declines and keeps working, Connor picks up a stick and throws it at the wood that Paul is stacking. Paul continues stacking the wood and only says, "Cut it out, Connor." Connor picks up another piece of wood and throws it directly at Paul. Paul stops his work, glares at Connor, and is about to say something when Jason intervenes, saying, "You heard what Paul said, son. Stop!"

Both boys are enjoying gathering the sticks, along with their informal contest. When Rob reminds them what the task is, Paul stops gathering the wood (response inhibition) and complies right away. He also continues to attend to this task (interference control) in spite of Connor's attempts to distract him from it. Response inhibition refers not only to behavior but to thoughts and emotions as well. When Paul declines Connor's plea to continue gathering wood, Connor responds aggressively. He is unable to inhibit either his emotional response (anger) or his subsequent behavioral response (throwing sticks). Even when Connor gets a clear signal from Paul ("Cut it out, Connor"), he does not interrupt the ongoing response. Connor does not inhibit any of his responses until his father intervenes. Unlike Paul, who has internal resources for controlling his thoughts and behavior, Connor needs external controls to help him behave in appropriate ways.

After the campsite is prepared, the entire group goes on a nature walk. Connor walks ahead with Rob and his son. Jason follows a little behind and listens to their conversation. They are discussing what wildlife they might see during the camping trip. Rob and his son tell Connor about another camping trip where they used binoculars and spotted some hawks. Connor responds by telling them, "My dad and I saw a bald eagle." Although this is untrue, Jason doesn't say anything. He doesn't want to embarrass Connor in front of the others. Connor's listeners are very interested and begin to ask him questions. Connor makes up more details and his story becomes increasingly unbelievable. He becomes visibly anxious about the tale he has concocted. Jason sees the other boy glance at Rob; he doesn't know what to make of Connor's tale. Rob changes the subject and the boys begin looking for raccoon prints in the dirt. Jason is relieved that the other boy didn't challenge Connor on his truthfulness.

When Connor heard that his friend saw a hawk, the idea of seeing a bald eagle just popped into his head (as he later explained to his father). Once Rob and his son begin asking for more details, Connor does not know how to handle the situation, so continues fabricating the story. He is unable to interrupt that response.

Back at the campsite, Jason invites Paul to come to the lake and fish with him and Connor. This is Paul's first experience with fishing, and Jason shows him how to bait his hook, set his cork, and cast his line. He instructs both boys to talk softly and "be patient." Connor casts his line over Paul's and tangles it. After they straighten the lines out and Paul is fishing again, Connor again casts his line over Paul's.

After the line is untangled for the second time, Paul says that he is going to move to a new spot. Connor starts to follow him, but Jason stops him, telling him that Paul is upset with Connor's carelessness and wants to fish by himself. Connor is remorseful and asks if he can tell Paul that he is sorry. Jason tells him he can, but to come back right away and to give Paul some time to himself. Connor complies.

Paul is annoyed with Connor's behavior but does not respond with anger (response inhibition). Paul comes up with an alternative solution to the problem (cognitive flexibility) when he decides to move to a new spot. Connor is initially unable to understand the reason for Paul's move, but when his father explains, Connor is finally able to put himself in Paul's place (cognitive flexibility) and respond with empathy. We can see that the problem is not that Connor is uncaring. It is just that he needs much more external support to achieve the same level of response inhibition and cognitive flexibility that Paul achieves so naturally (Table 3.2).

Connor and his dad rejoin the others at the campsite and the boys begin to run some races. Jason sees that, as with the fishing, Connor does a lot of things that annoy the other boys: pushing, name calling, and trying to change the rules in the middle of the game. At one point, Connor gets angry, quits the game, and goes down to the lake by himself.

When Connor returns to the campsite, the others are preparing for their cookout. Connor sees a pocketknife that one of the men has left on the table and picks it up, opens it, and begins to carve his initials into the table. Rob reprimands him. Connor throws the knife on the ground and stomps off. Jason follows him and talks with him, and he returns and apologizes for his behavior.

Connor is continually bombarded with stimuli (the physical environment, the actions of the other campers, and his own inner thoughts and feelings) and he has limited ability to interrupt his immediate response to any of it. His behavioral responses lead to reactions of displeasure from other people

TABLE 3.2. Comparison of Paul and Connor's Response Inhibition

	Paul	*Connor*
Task: Stopping yourself from doing the wrong thing **Entails** • Inhibiting the prepotent response • Interference control • Interrupting an ongoing response	**Inhibiting the prepotent response:** Is able to refrain from initiating inappropriate or undesired actions. For example, resists the urge to run down to the lake before setting up camp.	**Inhibiting the prepotent response:** Does not refrain from initiating actions that are against the group norms. For example, runs to the lake rather than setting up tents; picks up a knife belonging to someone else and begins to carve his initials into the table.
	Interference control: Does not respond to distractions or provocations. For example, does not respond aggressively to Connor's provocative behavior (throwing wood, tangling the fishing lines).	**Interference control:** Even when having fun playing games with his peers, has difficulty filtering out peripheral issues and his own emotions and impulsively engages in name calling, pushing, and attempting to change the rules.

	Interrupting an ongoing response: Is able to stop in order to switch gears. For example, stops gathering wood immediately upon request from the group leader; interrupts his fishing to move to a different spot when Connor is being disruptive.	Interrupting an ongoing response: Even when he receives signals that his behavior is inappropriate (when Paul tells him to stop throwing the wood, or when his walking companions question his story about the bald eagle), he does not interrupt the inappropriate response.
Response to consequences		At home, Connor's parents have found that he does not respond to direction and consequences as well as his younger sisters. During the camping trip, he is remorseful about behaviors when his father points out that they are inappropriate, but this does not appear to decrease subsequent inappropriate behaviors.

(continued)

TABLE 3.2. Continued

	Paul	Connor
External support	Needs only age-appropriate external support in order to inhibit responses (e.g., a reminder from Rob that they are supposed to be sorting and stacking the wood). Other than that, his response inhibition is internally directed.	Is able to refrain from initiating or escalating inappropriate behavior (squirting ketchup on another boy's plate, throwing marshmallows in the fire, making fun of another boy) only when his father remains in close proximity to him and reminds and redirects him. This level of support would be expected for a much younger child.

(such as the reprimand from Rob); Connor then responds to their reactions and his emotions escalate.

> Jason stays close to Connor the rest of the evening, inter-rupting and redirecting him when his behavior is inappro-priate (squirting ketchup on another boy's plate, throwing marshmallows in the fire, making fun of one of the boys). With Jason monitoring him so closely, Connor's behavior does not escalate and there are no more episodes of his get-ting angry and stomping off.

Connor's ability to inhibit socially unacceptable behavior is far below normal for his age group. Although he is chrono-logically the oldest boy in the group, his behavior is much less mature than that of the other boys. This is the first time that Jason has spent an extended period of time with Connor and other boys his age. At home, Connor has two younger sisters. Jason and his wife, Ginger, have found that the younger children are much more responsive to direction and discipline than Connor. Although in the past Jason mostly left discipline up to his wife, in the past year he has made it clear to Connor—in words and actions—that he will back up Ginger on disciplinary matters. To date, Jason has attributed the differences between Connor and his sisters to Connor's being "all boy." But seeing Connor with his peers is an eye opener. Jason feels both embarrassed by Connor's behavior and sorry for Connor. When he confronted his son about the bald eagle story, he saw that Connor was as surprised by his lie as Jason was. He could also see that Connor felt bad about having lied.

It seems to Jason that all of the older boys relate to Connor much as they do to the 5-year-olds—mostly tolerant but often annoyed and irritated. Ginger has been telling Jason for some time that she has noticed that other children are beginning to exclude their son from activities. Jason has told Ginger she is imagining things, that there is nothing wrong with Connor, but now he begins to suspect that he is the one who has imagined things to be different than they really are. He has wanted to believe that Connor will grow out of his behaviors. Seeing Connor with his peers brings back memories of Jason's own childhood. He too was very impulsive and always the one to get in trouble. These difficulties lasted well past high school, and Jason now reflects that his hope that Connor will outgrow these behaviors soon is probably unfounded. Jason has known that Connor is a lot like him, and he himself has often complained about Connor's lack of self-control, but this camping trip brings the seriousness of Connor's problem into sharp focus. He decides to talk with Ginger when he returns home and make a plan. If there is anything they can do to help, he doesn't want Connor to have to experience the same difficulties that he did.

Amanda: Shifting Focus

On a Wednesday morning in late September, Ms. Blum prepares the classroom for her 16 preschool students. There are nine girls and seven boys; most of them are 4 years old. Two of the girls are a bit of a challenge: Celia, who is strong willed, opinionated, and bossy with the other children; and Amanda, who is even more strong willed (often ignoring instructions from the teachers) and is very easily upset by things that the other children do. Sometimes Amanda, like Celia, is bossy, but just as often she avoids the other children or isolates herself. In spite of Celia's bossiness, the other children seem to like and even look up to her, but they often avoid Amanda, whose behavior can be aggressive and unpredictable.

> Celia is the first to arrive. She hangs her jacket neatly in her cubby, goes to the daily schedule posted on the wall, and asks Ms. Blum what they will do that day. This is Celia's usual routine. She likes to know exactly what to expect and during the day she frequently reminds Ms. Blum what comes next. (Ms. Blum jokes that Celia could probably take over in her absence: She knows the routine, knows where all the supplies are kept, and knows each of the children and their likes and dislikes, including who is allergic to peanuts and who is allergic to milk). After checking in with Ms. Blum, Celia stays near the cubbies, monitoring the other children to make sure that each one hangs his or her jacket in the right cubby. She becomes progressively more intrusive with the other children, telling Drew that he can't hang his jacket inside out. Drew stares at her and Ms. Blum intervenes, reminding Celia of the school rule: You can tell yourself what to do, but only the teachers can tell other children what to do.

As noted in Chapter 2, shifting focus is a multistep process: self-monitoring to determine if an ongoing response is appropriate and in one's best interest; interruption of the ongoing response if it is not; and cognitive flexibility, or considering alternative ways of perceiving or behaving. In a preschool class, children are not expected to be capable of self-monitoring. The children know the classroom rules but aren't always able to recognize (working memory) the need to apply them—especially to themselves—in the moment-by-moment flow of activities. Thus, preschool teachers spend a lot of time reminding their charges of the classroom rules, as Ms. Blum does with Celia. Once reminded, however, they are expected to be able to interrupt their ongoing response.

> Celia hesitates. Drew has left the cubby area but his jacket is still hanging inside out. Celia remains in front of his cubby, her eyes still fixed on the offending jacket.

Upon a reminder from her teacher, Celia is able to interrupt her response—she does not say anything else to Drew, nor does she touch the jacket. This shows progress from the beginning of the school year. Previously she persisted in her bossy behavior, but after being sent to time out on a couple of occasions, she learned to follow the rule when reminded. She is still unable, however, to shift her attention away from the cubbies.

> Ms. Blum tells Celia that it is Kate's turn to put out the carpet squares today. She suggests that Celia ask Kate if she would like some help. Celia turns her gaze from the jacket to Ms. Blum. Ms. Blum reminds Celia that it is up to Kate; if Kate doesn't want a helper, then Celia can read a book or draw a picture.

The next step in shifting focus is cognitive flexibility. As Celia stands fixedly in front of Drew's cubby, Ms. Blum gives her a little help with this final piece of the process: She suggests something she knows that Celia likes to do (set out the carpet squares) and at the same time reminds Celia that since that is actually Kate's job, she needs to be prepared to think flexibly—she also has the options of coloring or reading a book.

> Celia leaves to find Kate and asks to help her put out the carpet squares. When Kate tells Celia that she doesn't want any help, Celia starts to say, "You have to. . . ." However, she stops herself in midsentence and says instead, "Okay, then I'm going to go and color with Rose." With that information, Kate changes her mind and tells Celia, "Okay, you can help me and then I'll color with you."

Four-year-olds need a lot of external support from their teachers (hence the need for a smaller student-teacher ratio), and Celia is a good example of this. Had Ms. Blum not been nearby monitoring Celia's actions, Celia might have gotten into a tussle with Drew over his jacket. Celia was able to inhibit her desire to physically intervene, but she needed Ms. Blum's support to (1) remember that she was supposed to stop, and (2) flexibly shift her thoughts to other things. This is a developmentally appropriate amount of support for a 4-year-old. Moments later, perhaps because Ms. Blum's instructions are fresh in her mind, Celia is able to perform all three parts of shifting focus (self-monitoring, response inhibition, and thinking flexibly) in her interaction with Kate. She remembers the rule, stops herself from telling Kate what to do, and comes up with a different plan.

> Amanda arrives soon after Celia's departure from the cubby area. She goes to her cubby, hangs her jacket, and then goes straight to the book area. She has a favorite book, and she plans to begin her day doing the same thing that she did

yesterday and the day before: sit in the red beanbag chair and look at her book until circle time. When she arrives in the book area, she sees that Deidra is in the red beanbag chair. Amanda forgets momentarily about the book. "That's *my* chair," she tells Deidra, standing directly in front of her. Deidra looks up, then ignores Amanda and continues to look at her book. Amanda grabs Deidra's book and pulls, but Deidra holds on. Amanda begins to get louder: "You're in my chair!" Deidra replies in an equally loud voice, "Stop, Amanda!" Ms. Dartez, the assistant teacher, having witnessed the whole interchange, enters the book area and gets down on the floor with the girls. "Amanda, Deidra had that chair first. If you were there first, you would not want someone to make you move," she says in a calm and soothing voice. "You can sit in the blue chair."

Like Celia, Amanda often forgets the rules and has to be monitored by her teachers for compliance. But unlike Celia, who interrupted her response once reminded by Ms. Blum, Amanda does not interrupt her response when reminded by Ms. Dartez. Ms. Dartez attempts to help Amanda think more flexibly. First she encourages her to think of the situation from another point of view: "Deidra had that chair first. If you were there first, you would not want someone to make you move." Amanda is unresponsive to this approach and Ms. Dartez next helps her consider alternative solutions: "You can sit in the blue chair." But Amanda is still unable to interrupt her response and remains intent on ousting Deidra from the chair.

"No," says Amanda, now grabbing the edge of the red bean-bag, "that's *my* chair." Ms. Dartez leads Amanda away from the chairs, talking to her soothingly. Amanda stays with her but keeps her eyes fixed on Deidra.

Ms. Dartez has to physically disrupt Amanda's response by maneuvering her away from Deidra and the chair. Ms. Dartez tries to soothe her, but Amanda's attention remains focused on Deidra. Ms. Dartez can tell from Amanda's body language that she is still upset.

> Another girl comes up to Deidra and speaks to her. Deidra gets up, leaving the book on the chair, and follows the other girl to the coloring table. Amanda immediately pulls away from Ms. Dartez and seats herself in the red chair, holding the book that Deidra had left behind. She wants to get up and get her favorite book, but she doesn't want to leave the chair. She begins to cry.

Like the 4-year-olds in the Stanford study who were weak self-regulators (Chapter 1), Amanda remains in an aroused emotional state. Even with extensive support from Ms. Dartez, she is unable to interrupt her response (cognitive or behavioral) and is unable to shift her thoughts away from the red chair.

> Ms. Blum calls the children for circle time. All of the other children are already seated when Ms. Dartez arrives with Amanda, who is crying quietly because she never got to read her book. Ms. Dartez seats herself behind Amanda. Amanda often is physically intrusive with the children sitting beside her, and Ms. Dartez wants to be ready to intervene quickly, if needed. However, today Amanda is quiet, staring out the window and sucking two fingers of one hand as the other hand strokes the bottom edge of her T-shirt.

Amanda was unable to calm herself during the chair incident. Even after she was able to use the chair, she remained
in an aroused state. Now Ms. Dartez has physically shifted
her to a new activity, and Amanda regulates her emotions
with physical self-soothing behaviors.

Both Celia and Amanda are described as strong willed by
their teachers (Table 3.3). However, Celia has progressed a
lot since the beginning of the school year and is able to shift
her focus with minimal, age-appropriate reminders from her
teachers. Amanda, in contrast, is unable to shift focus even
with those reminders. She needs much more external support and direction, which often consists of physically moving
her from one place to another. She is able to soothe herself
eventually, but by immature means: sucking her fingers and
stroking her shirt.

Ms. Blum and Ms. Dartez have been consistent in giving
Amanda hints, in redirecting her, and in providing emotional
support when she gets upset. When Amanda's behavior is
aggressive or openly defiant, they use time out. However,
they have seen no progress. In some ways, Amanda's behavior appears to be getting worse. Ms. Blum has recently called
Amanda's parents and set up a meeting. She hopes that they
will be able to help find a solution for Amanda's difficult behaviors.

Marcus: Goal Orientation

Susan and Al have recently met with Ms. Washington,
their son Marcus's second grade teacher. Ms.Washington in-
formed them that 7-year-old Marcus is falling behind the rest
of the children in the class. He does not complete inde-

TABLE 3.3. Comparison of Celia and Amanda's Ability to Shift Focus

	Celia	Amanda
Task: Making yourself stop thinking about one thing so you can start thinking about (and then do) something else. **Entails** • Working memory • Response inhibition • Cognitive flexibility	**Working memory/response inhibition:** Needs an age-appropriate reminder from her teacher to cue her working memory regarding the classroom rules. Once she is reminded, she inhibits her behavior in keeping with the rule. For example, stops herself from interfering with Drew upon reminder from the teacher. **Cognitive flexibility:** Needs age-appropriate suggestion from her teacher to help her think about other things to do (help Kate with the carpet squares, color, read a book). With the suggestion, is able to follow through very competently.	**Working memory/response inhibition:** Even with reminders about the classroom rules, is unable to inhibit her responses. For example, does not stop her inappropriate response to Deidra's presence in the red chair even when reminded by the teacher. **Cognitive flexibility:** Even with suggestions from the teacher, is not able to think about the situation differently and continues to focus on only one alternative: removing Deidra from the red chair.

(continued)

TABLE 3.3. Continued

	Celia	Amanda
Response to discipline	Earlier in the year, persisted in bossy behavior with other children. However, after being sent to time out on a couple of occasions, she started responding to reminders from the teaching staff and was able to consistently follow the rules.	Reminders, redirections, and multiple time outs have not brought about any changes in problem behaviors.
External support	Is considered strong willed by her teachers, but is able to respond to reminders and suggestions. The level of support is age appropriate for a preschool child.	Verbal reminders and suggestions (and age-appropriate level of support) are not sufficient. Often needs physical intervention to inhibit ongoing behavior and even then has a difficult time thinking flexibly about events.

pendent seat work, she says, unless she stands right next to him and makes sure he does it. Susan acknowledges that Marcus often gets off track in doing schoolwork, and she tells Ms. Washington that in first grade his teacher had used a buddy system. Marcus was paired with another student, which seemed to help him stay on track. She mentions that the first grade teacher said that Marcus's completed work was often more correct than that of his buddy, as his actual knowledge of the material was usually quite good.

Ms. Washington lets Susan and Al know that this year she expects Marcus to work independently. She understands that it takes a while for students to adjust to this new expectation, but it is already November. The other students are making the transition to independent work, but Marcus is not. He is quite capable, she says, but he doesn't seem to care about his school performance. Ms. Washington hints to Susan and Al that if their son does not show some improvement, he might not pass second grade.

After that meeting, Marcus's parents decide to use a system of rewards and punishments to try to influence their son to show more effort at school. They sit down with him and explain that he has to be more responsible. They promise that if he brings home good reports during the week, he will have special rewards on the weekend; but if not, he will lose the privileges, including video games, TV programs, and visiting with friends on weekends. Marcus is happy about the prospect of earning special rewards. The family even makes a menu of rewards that he will be able to choose from. Marcus promises to try harder in school and their talk ends on a happy note.

Three weeks later, on a Thursday morning in late November, Ms. Washington passes out worksheets to the class. She then stands in front of the students, holds up a copy of the worksheet, and explains what to do. She points to a list of five nouns at the top of the sheet. This is followed by five sentences, each with a blank space. "Read the first sentence," she tells the class, "and decide which noun fits in that sentence. Write that noun in the blank space. Then cross out that noun in the list at the top, because you can't use it again. Then read the next sentence, and choose the noun that fits in that sentence. Don't forget to cross it out at the top before you go to the next sentence. When you finish all five, turn your paper over and take out your reading book."

Ms. Washington sees her job as helping her students make the transition from first grade, where they were still to some extent "babied," to third grade, where they will need to be capable of independent work. For today's assignment, she expects her students to have the right materials on their desks, remain seated as they work quietly at their worksheets, and raise a hand if they need help. When their work is completed, she expects them to turn the paper over, take out their reading book, and read quietly until she calls for their papers. As she gives her instructions, she looks out at her students, all of whom have their eyes on her. Andrew, one of her best students, alternates between looking at her and looking down at his worksheet.

As Andrew listens to his teacher's instructions, he glances down at his worksheet and begins to picture himself completing the task. When she gives the final instruction, he pictures himself taking out his reading book, and he anticipates the sense of satisfaction that he will feel. Andrew reads the directions at the top of his worksheet, providing himself with a written reminder of his teacher's instructions. Next, he reads the list of five words. He tells himself, "I need to choose the right word for each sentence."

Goal orientation is the ability to make a plan for achieving a goal and then holding that information in mind while activating and executing all its aspects. Andrew not only listens to Ms. Washington's instructions, he also reads the written instructions and commits himself to a specific plan of action: "I need to choose the right word for each sentence." He is essentially using the "when-then" format of goal formulation (see Chapter 2), telling himself that when there is an empty space, then he needs to choose the right word.

Andrew reads the first sentence, looks back at the list of nouns, chooses the correct word, and writes it in the blank. He crosses that word off the list. "That's one finished," he tells himself. He reads the next item, chooses a word, and writes it in the blank space. "That's two—only three left."

He uses self-directed language to monitor his progress and motivate himself, by saying things such as, "That's one finished." He is simultaneously performing interference control, filtering out distractions in the classroom—other children asking for help, getting up and sharpening their pencils, and so on.

When Andrew gets to the last sentence, four words are crossed out and there is one word left. He reads the last sentence and realizes that the remaining word will not make sense in that sentence. He raises his hand, and when Ms. Washington comes to his desk, he explains his problem.

Although Andrew is intent on completing the worksheet, he is able to shift focus as needed.

The combination of an internalized plan of action and an ability to monitor his progress keeps him focused on filling in each blank with the correct word. He does not look up from the task until he meets an obstacle. Even then, he does not lose sight of his goal of using each word in one (and only one) of the blanks. Unable to meet the goal on his own, he asks for help.

Ms. Washington helps Andrew recognize that he used the incorrect word on item 3. He erases that word in the sentence. Ms. Washington prompts him to erase the word he crossed out on the list of nouns as well. She then walks away. Andrew then enters the correct word in item 3 and crosses that word off the list. He is now able to complete the last item. "I'm finished," he says to himself as he crosses out the final noun. He looks around the room. Two other students appear to have finished their worksheets, but most are still writing. "I'm one of the first ones finished," he says to himself. He feels a sense of satisfaction as he takes out his reading book.

Help received, Andrew completes the task, and then acknowledges the completion of the goal by saying to himself, "I'm finished." He also monitors his performance by comparing his progress to that of other students. He has not only met the goal of selecting the correct word for each blank; he has done so in a timely manner.

Across the room, as Marcus listens to Ms. Washington's instructions, he too begins to imagine an outcome for the activity. He forms an internal image of his teacher being pleased with him. While she is still speaking, he recalls that just yesterday she praised him for forming his letters neatly. He feels happy as he remembers her praise, recalling her smile, her words, his feeling of satisfaction.

Unlike Andrew, Marcus does not immediately visualize a plan of action that is specific to completing today's worksheet. Instead, he recalls the sensation of Ms. Washington being pleased with him in the past and recalls past actions (neat handwriting) related to her praise. He spends time just enjoying the recall of this past event.

After a bit, Marcus looks around, sees the other students busy writing, and recalls that Ms. Washington said to use the five words at the top of the page to fill in the blanks in the sentences below. He says to himself, "I need to write the words neatly in the blank spaces." He chooses a word at random and, as he carefully forms the letters in the first blank, he says to himself, "That's the way Ms. Washington likes them."

The plan of action that he eventually formulates—to gain his teacher's approval through neat handwriting—is insufficient to the task at hand. He does not read the written instructions on the worksheet, so he has no external prompt that might help him correct his action plan. Like Andrew, he uses internalized language to motivate himself ("That's the way Ms. Washington likes them") but since his goal is imprecise, the internalized language is not helping him meet the expectations of this particular task.

TABLE 3.4. Comparison of Andrew and Marcus's Goal Orientation

	Andrew	Marcus
Task: Making a good plan for what you are going to do and then following your plan and getting it done on time. Entails • Planning • Self-monitoring • Time management	Planning: Begins to create an internalized plan of action while teacher is giving verbal instruction. Plan of action ("I need to choose the best word for each sentence") correlates accurately with the demands of the present task: Provides himself with external support for his plan of action by reading directions on worksheet.	Planning: Does not create a plan of action while teacher is giving verbal instruction. Plan of action ("I need to write the words neatly in the blanks") does not correlate accurately with the demands of the present task. Does not read written instructions, therefore does not have any external check or support for his internalized plan.

Self-monitoring and time management: Uses the self-correcting nature of the worksheet (crossing out words after using them) to monitor adherence to plan of choosing the best word for each sentence. When he is unable to adhere to his plan, he shifts focus and asks for help.

Uses internalized language to monitor progress in terms of timely goal completion. ("That's two finished, only three left.")

Self-monitoring and time management: The self-correcting nature of the worksheet is useless to him, as his plan of action (writing the words neatly) does not include choosing the correct word for each sentence. Does not realize he is off track until teacher comes and takes his paper away.

Does not use internalized language to monitor performance in terms of timely goal completion. Only the intermittent awareness of other children moving ahead prompts him to move along more quickly.

(*continued*)

TABLE 3.4. Continued

	Andrew	Marcus
Response to consequences		Parents work with him and set up system of rewards (and losing privileges) at home. He is enthusiastic about the program, but it has no effect on his schoolwork.
External support	Needs external support only once during assignment, for the content of the material, not for the executive function of goal orientation.	Can reliably carry out assignment only when paired with another student with strong goal orientation or when teacher stands by his desk and monitors him.

With the first item complete, Marcus looks around the room again. Paul asks permission to sharpen his pencil and Marcus watches as Paul uses the sharpener, returns to his seat, and begins writing. Marcus decides that he should sharpen his pencil also.

Marcus's ability to self-monitor is also weak. He does not monitor his behavior based on any internal standard; instead he uses an intermittent awareness of what other children are doing. In this case, he becomes aware of another child sharpening his pencil, which prompts him to do the same.

Marcus asks for, and receives, permission to sharpen his pencil. On his way back to his seat, he notes that Rebecca has crossed out three of the words at the top of the page. He recalls that Ms. Washington said to cross out each noun after using it.

Again, it is only the sight of the other child's actions that prompts him to monitor his own performance. His new awareness that Rebecca has crossed out three words orients him to the goal of using all of the words at the top of the worksheet.

Back at his seat, Marcus crosses out the noun that he used in the first sentence and moves to the second item. He chooses a noun from the list and writes it neatly in the blank space, forming the letters precisely with his newly sharpened pencil. "That looks good," he says to himself. With that item complete, he looks up again. Ms. Washington is talking with Andrew, and Andrew erases one of his answers. Marcus looks down at his own neatly lettered words and feels proud; he won't need to erase and rewrite his.

When Marcus looks up again, all of his classmates have opened their reading books. His feeling of satisfaction begins to fade as he recalls that Ms. Washington has been displeased in the past when he works too slowly. He also remembers that his parents will not be happy that he didn't complete his worksheet.

Since their meeting with Ms. Washington—and subsequent talk with Marcus—3 weeks ago, Susan and Al have stuck by the plan they created with Marcus. Marcus has not earned a single reward. He has, however, lost his video and TV privileges. All weekend outings with friends have been canceled. Just last night, his parents reminded him of his promise to try harder, and Marcus said he would. Susan even reminded him this morning to pay attention, do what Ms. Washington says, and get his work done. Marcus promised her that he would do better today.

Ms. Washington approaches Marcus's desk and takes away his worksheet. She says that he will have to stay in at recess to complete the worksheet. It is obvious that she is disappointed with him, and Marcus feels sad. He thinks about staying in at recess. He will miss the kickball game with his friends, but he looks forward to having Ms. Washington's undivided attention.

However, at recess, Ms. Washington simply returns his worksheet and busies herself at her desk. She is determined that Marcus will learn to work independently this year. She writes a note to send home with Marcus.

In her note, Ms. Washington informs Marcus's parents that he is still not paying attention, still not completing his work.

She again tells them he must learn to work independently if he is to progress to third grade. She asks that they please "talk with Marcus about this."

That evening, Susan reads Ms. Washington's note to Al and they begin to argue about what they should do next. Clearly the system of rewards and punishments that they had been so optimistic about a few weeks ago is not helping. Susan wonders if perhaps Ms. Washington is right: Perhaps Marcus just doesn't care. Al reminds her that Marcus did fine in school last year. He suggests that they enroll Marcus in a different school. Susan counters that she does not want to move Marcus without moving his older sister, Olivia. But Olivia is having a great year and it seems unfair to make her move.

Susan suggests that they increase the punishment. They have taken away all of his electronic entertainment and his weekend outings with friends. Perhaps they should also take away soccer and basketball, which he loves dearly. Al becomes angry with her for even suggesting this, and Susan begins to cry. Al then begins to vent anger toward Ms. Washington. She has taken a simple school problem, he says, and created problems for their home.

Thirty minutes later, still at a stalemate over what to do next, Susan and Al decide to consult with Marcus's pediatrician. The pediatrician had been Susan's doctor as a child and they trust her guidance and judgment.

Helping Children Meet Expectations: Finding the Right Level of Support

Marcus's story—like those of Jon, Connor, and Amanda—is typical: a child appears to be falling behind his peers in some behavioral expectation such as following directions, thinking before acting, keeping hands to oneself, or working independently. In each of these cases, concerned adults—Jon's mother, Connor's father, Amanda's teachers, Marcus's parents—first intervened by utilizing discipline, or various systems of positive and negative consequences, to influence the child's behavior. As with Marcus's parents, the adults often begin to feel frustrated, angry, and unsure of who or what is to blame for the problem.

In providing counseling for children and parents, we certainly see some parents who lack either the knowledge or the will to use an appropriate and consistent program of discipline with their child, resulting in behavior problems. Teaching those parents about behavior management, or helping them to more reliably execute a behavior management plan, can bring about the desired changes in the child's behavior. However, there are also many cases where the adults are already consistently following a solid behavior management program and there are no changes in the child's behavior.

While a consistent system of reward and punishment may work for a child who is lacking structure and motivation, it will not be effective if the child has not acquired the underlying competencies that allow for self-regulation. In fact, continuing to rely on such a system may lead to a sense of helplessness for the child and the parents as well. (And a sense of helplessness is the opposite of the result that we want to achieve: the sense of mastery that comes with the use of self-directed strategies to achieve one's goals.) For those children, intervention needs to move to the next level, improving the underlying capacity for self-regulation. We have found two ways to do this: (1) providing *co-regulation*, and

(2) enlisting the child in planning and utilizing self-regulation strategies (Table 3.5).

As each example in this chapter has demonstrated, parents and other concerned individuals often intuitively offer external support to compensate for the child's difficulties with self-regulation. Jon's mother structured the morning routine in a way that compensated for his poor working memory. Connor's father stayed close by him at the campout in order to inhibit and redirect inappropriate responses. Amanda's teacher physically moved her during upsetting events. Marcus's first grade teacher provided a buddy to help him stay oriented to the goals of classroom assignments. These people were providing co-regulation for the child. While effective, the downsides of co-regulation are that (1) the adult has to be present at the point of performance to provide the support, and (2) both adult and child are aware that the child's peers don't need this level of support and both would prefer for the child to be able to function more independently. When Mia provided co-regulation—by setting Jon's alarm clock, laying out his clothes, setting the timer at breakfast, and reminding him to brush his teeth and comb his hair—her external support ensured that he would be ready to go when Pierre arrived at 7:00 A.M. But this external support did not improve Jon's self-regulation. In contrast, when Jon learned to use a wrist list to plan and carry out his chores, he was engaging in self-regulation. This was an empowering and motivating experience for him.

In Part II, we look at executive function from a developmental perspective. How does it develop internally? What external factors nurture this development? How can we understand the needs of children who seem to fall behind their

TABLE 3.5. Levels of Intervention

Intervention	Underlying assumption	Example
Discipline (behavior management)	Child is assumed to have normal capacity for self-regulation. Behavior management program motivates the child to act on that capacity.	Pierre's mother tells him that he has to be ready for school before he can spend time with his stepfather in the morning. With this motivation, Pierre quickly learns to perform all of the required actions in a timely fashion.
Coregulation	Child's capacity for self-regulation is weak. An adult provides one-on-one support at the point of performance.	Jon's mother provides cues and reminders to help him be ready for school on time.
Empowering children to become more self-directed	Child's capacity for self-regulation is weak. Child learns self-directed strategies for improving performance.	Jon learns to use a wrist list to plan and carry out his Saturday chores.

peers in meeting expectations? Then, in Part III, we return to the stories of Jon, Connor, Amanda, and Marcus and see how carefully planned and developmentally sensitive external support helped these children grow in their ability to intentionally regulate their thoughts, emotions, and actions.

PART II

A Developmental Perspective

CHAPTER FOUR

A Natural Progression

How Self-Regulation Is Internalized

IN CHAPTER 1, WE considered the difficulty that 10-year-old Jon and some of the Stanford 4-year-olds (Mischel et al., 1989) experienced in bringing their actions in line with their intentions. Their actions—rather than following their intentions—were influenced primarily by their immediate perceptual field, by what they experienced in the here and now: the sight of the treat in the case of the 4-year-olds and the actions of his dog in the case of Jon. In contrast, the Stanford 4-year-olds who acted intentionally were able to do so because their actions were directed by internal ideas rather than their immediate perceptual field.

How do children learn to subordinate their actions to their thoughts and thus acquire the option of acting independently of their immediate experience? This subordination is the essence of executive function, so understanding how it occurs in a child's development will give us a basis for understanding how we may strengthen executive function for children who have difficulty with self-regulation.

Self-Regulation Moves from External to Internal

Executive functions begin to develop during infancy and continue into late adolescence—a lengthy period. The most rapid development, however, takes place during the preschool years—approximately ages 3 to 5 (Center on the Developing Child, 2011). Self-regulation develops on many fronts—cognitive, emotional, behavioral—and, according to many researchers, this development follows a universal pattern. Executive functions exist first, during early childhood, in shared and external forms of interaction and gradually become converted to private and internal mental tools.

According to Russell Barkley, executive functions originate in external, more public behaviors that function initially "to sense and to control the outer world" (1997, p. 209). Over time, these behaviors are turned toward the self as a means of informing and controlling one's own behavior. In the process the behaviors lose their outward, publicly observable manifestations and are said to be internalized (Barkley, 1997). Lev Vygotsky, a Russian psychologist and contemporary of the French psychologist Jean Piaget, made a similar observation decades earlier. Vygotsky theorized that these brain functions (which he termed *higher mental functions*) begin in shared activities and then become appropriated by the individual and transformed for internal use, guiding the child toward more effective self-regulation of thoughts, emotions, and behavior.

While this internalization process continues over many years, because of the big leap it takes during preschool years, it is particularly easy to view the process during this developmental period. In this chapter, using the example of a young child named Chloe, we examine the movement from externalized to internalized forms of regulation in two areas of development that are central to the toddler and preschool years: language and play.

Language and Self-Regulation

Language is social in origin. In the young child's life, speech exists first as a means of communication with others. It begins with others directing language toward the infant.

While she is an infant, Chloe's mother, father, and brother talk with her often, describing objects ("See the doggie? What a nice doggie. Pet the doggie, Chloe. Such a soft doggie"), introducing activities ("Let's go for a walk. Let's put on your shoes. Here's your stroller. Let's go"), and conversing with her even if Chloe's only contribution to the dialogue is baby talk. ("Should we have mashed potatoes for dinner, Chloe? . . . Ma-ma-ma-ma? . . . Yes, that's a good idea. Mama will fix some mashed potatoes for dinner.")

When Chloe is a bit older, her family uses language to monitor and guide her actions. ("No, Chloe, don't pull the dog's tail. Let's put your hat on, Chloe, so we can go to the store. Give Grandma a kiss, Chloe. The stove is hot, Chloe; don't touch.")

In similar fashion, the child learns to use language to share her perceptions with others and also to try to influence the behavior of others and the course of events. When she says, "Baba," Chloe is communicating that she wants her mother to give her a bottle. When she says, "Doggie nice," Chloe shares her perception that the dog is friendly. When she says, "No hat! No go!" Chloe is trying to influence her family not to make her put on her hat and go to the store.

As Chloe becomes more capable of doing things for herself, shared language can help her improve her performance. When Chloe attempts to put on her own socks, she is only able to pull them as far as her heel. She walks around with her heels bare and the socks flopping in front of her toes. She sits and attempts to pull them further, without success. Her mother observes her struggle and uses language to introduce strategies that make the process easier.

"Look, Chloe, the sock has a toe and a heel. Here's the toe of the sock," her mother says as she scrunches up the sock, making the toe more accessible. "Put your toes in the toe of the sock first." Chloe places her toes in the toe of the sock. Her mother then pulls the sock as far as her heel. "Here's the heel of the sock. Your heel goes here." Her mother pulls the sock so that it barely covers Chloe's heel. "Now you can pull up your sock, Chloe." Chloe pulls the sock into place, pleased. "Good job, Chloe," her mother says. "Now let's put the other one on. Toe first, then heel." Her mother repeats the process of putting Chloe's sock on as far as her heel, using language to explain the strategy. Chloe again gives it the final pull into place. "Good job, Chloe. You put your toes here and your heel there, right where they belong."

Chloe probably does not understand all of what her mother is saying, but the next time Chloe is struggling with her socks, her mother, says, "Remember, toe first." This shared language supports Chloe's working memory and reminds her that there is a strategy for putting on her socks. She still needs help getting the process started, and her mother repeats the language, in abbreviated form, each time as she demonstrates and assists. Eventually Chloe is able to manage the task with only verbal assistance: "Remember, Chloe: toe, heel, pull."

Private Speech

In the above examples, language is external and is used for communication between individuals. According to Vygotsky, at around the age of 2 years children begin to use language in another way. They turn social speech (speech directed toward others) inward toward the self, and use self-directed language to plan, monitor, and guide their own activities.

As Chloe's working memory develops, she uses her mother's language to direct herself as she puts on her socks, telling herself "pull" when she gets to the hard part of maneuvering the sock over her heel. As she approaches a hot oven, Chloe says to herself, "No, don't touch, hot." She has heard these instructions directed toward her before. But now Chloe is verbally directing her own actions. By bringing her behavior under the control of internally represented forms of information, she has less need of external regulation.

Speech makes a child less impulsive. Chloe may have eventually figured out how to put on her own socks using trial and error. But in using language to guide the process, she has also learned a strategy for planned, rather than spontaneous, action. Her mother has shown her that activity can be divided into two parts: first, figuring out how to solve the problem through language, and second, carrying out the solution through action. "Direct manipulation is replaced by a complex psychological process through which inner motivations and intentions, postponed in time, stimulate their own development and realization" (Vygotsky, 1978, p. 26).

Speech not only facilitates the child's effective manipulation of objects and the environment, but also provides a means of regulating the child's perceptions, emotions, and behavior.

> As a toddler, Chloe spills her milk. Her older brother yells, "Chloe, you made a mess!" Chloe bursts into tears. Her mother intervenes, saying, "It's okay, sweetie, we'll get a rag and wipe it up." She gets two rags and gives Chloe one. "You can help, Chloe. Let's clean up the milk." Chloe stops crying and wipes the rag on the floor. "See, Chloe," her mother says, "it's okay. We made it all better. It's okay now." Chloe smiles and repeats, "It's okay."

In this shared interaction, her mother has used shared language to help Chloe change her perception of the situation and thus to transform her emotions. A week after the spilled-milk incident, Chloe again spills a drink. She initially looks distressed. But then she repeats her mother's soothing language from the previous experience, saying aloud to herself, "It's okay, Chloe. Wipe it up. Don't cry." As she goes to get a towel, her affect changes from distressed to cheerful. She is using private speech for self-regulation.

In using language for self-direction and self-soothing, the young child initially speaks aloud to herself as if to another person. As noted in Chapter 2, Berk (1994) has studied this "private speech" and found that it accounts for 20% to 60% of the spoken language of preschool-age children. As a child gains mastery over behavior, private speech abbreviates and becomes less audible.

A year later, Chloe is even more adept at using language to resolve problems. During a play activity, her cousin Sarah calls Chloe a baby. Chloe is upset, but rather than reacting immediately as she did to her brother's comment when she was a toddler, she leaves the play, goes to her mother, and tells her what Sarah said.

Mother: Do you know any babies?
Chloe: Lucy's a baby.
Mother: How do you know Lucy is a baby?
Chloe: She's little.
Mother: What else makes her a baby?
Chloe: She drinks out of a bottle.
Mother: Anything else?
Chloe: She wears a diaper.
Mother: So a baby is little, drinks out of a bottle, and wears a diaper, right?
Chloe: Yes.
Mother: Are you little like Lucy? Do you drink out of a bottle? Do you wear a diaper?
Chloe: No!
Mother: Well then, if Sarah thinks you're a baby, how silly is Sarah?
Chloe: Sarah is silly!
Mother: Tell Sarah, "Don't be silly!"

Satisfied, Chloe returns to her play. The next time Sarah calls her a baby, Chloe says, "Don't be silly, Sarah." Sarah doesn't respond. Their play continues, and there are no more instances of Sarah calling Chloe a baby.

Chloe has learned that language is a tool that can help her manage difficult situations. In this particular situation, she cannot figure out by herself how to use language to soothe her upset feelings, but she knows from previous shared interactions that language can help. So she goes to her mother, and her mother shares a problem-solving approach using language to come up with a way to perceive the situation. Chloe's new perception of the situation alters her emotions and subsequent behavior.

Less than a year later, 4-year-old Chloe is able to use language independently to manage her perception of a problem situation. She is playing in the neighbor's yard with 5-year-old Casey and 6-year-old Ian. She leaves the swing set and starts to get on a bicycle.

> "Girls can't ride bikes," says Casey. Chloe appears upset, hesitates, and looks to Ian for support, but he ignores the situation. "Girls can't ride bikes," Casey repeats. Chloe sits down and is quiet for a moment, gazing off. A moment later, she gets on the bike. "I told you girls can't ride bikes!" says Casey. "I'm a girl and I can ride a bike. Watch this!" says Chloe as she pedals off. The boys watch her and then Casey gets on a bike and joins her.

Presented with this problem situation, Chloe is upset, but she does not respond immediately as she did when she was a toddler. In the space provided by this response inhibition, she first seems to seek some external support (such as she received from her mother in the past) from Ian. When external support is not forthcoming, Chloe turns inward. She sits down by herself and gazes off. We can assume from her subsequent behavior that, in this space, she has talked to herself much as her mother has talked with her in the past, applying logic to the current situation. As Berk (2002) noted, once cognitive operations become well practiced, children start to "think words" rather than saying them.

In these examples, we can see Chloe's gradual progression in internalizing what were originally shared problem-solving activities. As a toddler, it is only with external support from her mother that Chloe is able to (1) interrupt her ongoing response to a problem (crying in response to her brother's comments about the spilled drink), and (2) use language to perceive the problem differently. At age 4, when no external support is available, she is able to independently delay her response to the problem (her friend's comment that girls can't ride bikes) and use language to regulate her perception and emotions. A strategy that originated in shared activity with her mother has been appropriated for private, internal use: the capacity to converse with oneself in a conscious, quasi-dialogic fashion in the course of everyday life (Barkley, 1997).

Internalized Language Is an Integral Part of Executive Function

Self-directed language provides the child with a mental tool that allows her to be more independent from the stimulation provided by the immediate, physical situation in which she finds herself. Self-directed language serves to open up the internal space between an initial stimulus and one's response, allowing the child to include stimuli that do not lie in the immediate visual field (Vygotsky, 1978). In the Stanford experiments, this is what the impulsive 4-year-olds learned to do in the second round of experiments: by thinking about the stimuli in a different way, or by thinking about something else, they were able to respond differently to the evocative stimulus (the tasty treat). Other tools derived from language can also serve the same purpose. For example, when Jon creates a wrist list for his chores, he is less influenced by his immediate external environment. The list is a visual and mental tool–self-directed language in external form–that provides stimuli that help Jon to direct his actions toward his goal.

Vygotsky theorized that the mental tools associated with language development help to build the cognitive skills that underlie self-regulation, such as behavioral inhibition, focused attention, deliberate memory, and problem solving. Modern research supports this theory, indicating that internalized language is an integral part of executive functions such as working memory, response inhibition, and cognitive flexibility (Berk, 1994; Berk & Potts, 1991; Gawrilow et al., 2011; Miyake et al., 2004). The more complex the action demanded by the situation and the less direct its resolution, the greater the role played by internalized language.

This movement from shared language to private speech and then internalized language provides the preschooler with powerful tools with which she can begin to regulate her memory, perceptions, and behavior. She will eventually integrate these language tools with a central activity of early childhood–play. This will provide her with ever more powerful experiences of self-regulation.

Play and Self-Regulation

The movement from external to internal forms of regulation can also be observed in the changes that take place in children's play as they mature. If we look closely at the lives of preschoolers, we can see that the play activities in which they are so happily engaged are actually workshops for building these higher mental functions.

During infancy, play is first directed outward.

At the age of 14 months, Chloe's favorite toy is a set of blocks. She sits with them for extended periods of time, putting them into the plastic storage box, dumping them out, and then doing it all over again. Her older brother recently stacked her blocks and then showed her how to knock the stack over. She delights in this new game. She initially knocked down the tower after her brother built it, but she now attempts to build the tower herself.

Chloe is learning new ways to manipulate the blocks and to experiment with their physical properties. Just a few months ago, she mostly mouthed the blocks and banged them together or on the coffee table. Before long she will be able to sort the blocks by color and size. In all these activities, she is reacting to and playing with the concrete physical properties of the blocks. However, in less than a year, she experiments with using the blocks in a radically different way.

At a little over 2 years of age, Chloe still enjoys playing with her blocks, but now she also plays with her doll, imitating the caretaking actions of her parents: pushing it in a stroller, tucking it into its miniature bed, trying to change its clothes. On this day, she is playing with her doll. Her blocks are nearby in their storage box. She observes her father as he ends a conversation on his phone and puts the phone down on the table. Chloe goes to the box of blocks, picks one up, and puts it to her ear. Her father notices this action. He smiles at Chloe as he picks up his phone and puts it to his ear. "Hello, Chloe," he says. "Is that you, Chloe?" She nods her head.

In this activity, Chloe initiates a use of the block that is completely different from the way she has previously used blocks. She knows that the block is not a phone, but she is acting as if it is. Now her actions are related to her inner idea of what a phone is rather than to the immediate physical reality of the block. In Vygotsky's terms, Chloe is engaging in higher mental functions.

Up until this time, Chloe's actions have been integrally tied to her sensory impressions. She reacts to the sight of food or the actions of a dog: Each perception is a stimulus to which she responds. Even when she inhibits a response, as she does with the hot stove or the spilled milk, her actions are directly linked to the external situation. She is therefore "constrained by the situation in which she finds herself" (Vygotsky, 1978, p. 96). But when she engages in this imaginary play, external factors begin to lessen their hold on her.

When Chloe sees one thing—a block—but reacts to an internal idea of a phone rather than only to the external attributes of the block, she begins to be able "to act independently of what she sees" (Vygotsky, 1978, p. 97). Her behavior in this moment is a deliberate attempt to solve a problem: She wants to imitate her father's actions but does not have a toy phone available. Rather than directing her behavior outward to aspects of the environment that are the most perceptually obvious (for example, trying to use her father's phone), she directs her attention inward to solve the problem (Bodrova & Leong, 2007). When Chloe uses her thoughts as mental tools to solve a problem, her behavior is no longer controlled just by external reality; she is acting in correspondence with internal ideas. She is not just playing with objects; she is playing with ideas. This is a huge step. With this new level of cognitive flexibility, she is on the road to self-regulating her behavior in more complex ways.

> "What are you doing, Chloe?" her father continues. "Are you taking care of your baby?" Chloe says yes, still holding the block to her ear. "Does your baby like to read stories?" Chloe nods again. "Why don't you bring your baby over here and I'll read you both a story," her father suggests, still speaking into his phone. Chloe picks up her doll and brings it to her father, still holding the block. "Do you want to put your phone here on the table by mine?" Chloe puts her block on the table and snuggles in to read a story.

Chloe's father observes her new use of the block and encourages her to expand this creative play, by engaging in a conversation with her and acting as if this conversation is taking place by phone.

> When the story is finished, her father makes a ringing sound and picks up Chloe's "phone," looks at it, pretends to turn it on, and says, "It's Mommy calling you." He hands the block to Chloe and she puts it to her ear. Her father prompts her: "Say hi to Mommy, Chloe." "Hi, Mommy," Chloe says. "Tell her what we just did," her father says, pointing to the book. "Book," Chloe says. "Is mommy still at the store?" her father inquires. Chloe doesn't respond. "Okay, hang up your phone now. Mommy has to drive," says her father, putting out his hand for the block. He pretends to turn it off and puts it on the table next to his phone.

Chloe's father takes the creative play one step further here, by pretending to carry on a conversation with someone who is not physically present. While Chloe is able to act as if she is talking to her mother (by repeating things that her father suggests), she is not able to imagine both sides of the conversation (for example, Mommy saying that she is still shopping). Nevertheless, Chloe has made a big developmental step forward on this day, and it won't be long before this type of play —playing with internally represented ideas—becomes a regular part of her day. Through this new type of play, Chloe will develop her mental tools in increasingly sophisticated ways.

Cooperative Play With Peers

Although Chloe's father may view his interactions with Chloe as "just play," research shows that this type of early play with caregivers helps prepare the child for later pretend play with peers (Haight & Miller, 1993). This cooperative play with peers will move the preschool child even further along the road to self-regulation. In order to engage in joint play, preschoolers have to utilize advanced executive functions such as planning, working memory, behavioral inhibition, self-monitoring, and cognitive flexibility. Preschool programs are one setting in which that cooperative play with peers can flourish.

> At age 4, Chloe attends preschool. On this day, she, Diego, and Carly have decided to play house. They have a play kitchen, a table and chair set, and some pots, pans, plates, bowls, and cups. Carly suggests that they cook a meal, and the others agree. They gather some checkers and small blocks to use as food.

At age 4, all of these children are now adept at responding to inner ideas (using checkers and blocks as food) rather than just external reality (checkers as game pieces and blocks as building materials). As noted above, when children act as if an object is something else, they have to inhibit or override their normal response to these items. The same is true when they react to one another's roles rather than to their real-life status.

> The children now assign roles. Chloe says that she wants to be the mother and Diego wants to be the father. Chloe and Diego suggest that Carly be the baby. Carly is willing to be the big sister, but not the baby. All three children want to have a baby in the play. They try to enlist another child for the role but have no takers. Their teacher notices their actions and comes over to see what is going on. She suggests that they use a doll as a baby. "No," says Chloe, "I want a baby who can really move and talk." The teacher suggests that Chloe could talk for the baby and shows her how to pretend that the doll is talking, by using a "baby voice" that is different than a "mother voice." Chloe and Diego look a bit unsure, but Carly immediately understands this idea. Carly takes the doll, makes it talk, and says that she will be both the big sister and the baby. She demonstrates her big sister voice and her baby voice. Chloe is satisfied with this solution and the teacher leaves the play area.

The teacher notices that the children's play has hit a snag and intervenes, giving their problem solving enough support so that they are able to resolve the issue and move on with their play. The solution that she offers—one child enacting multiple roles—takes their play to a new level of complexity.

Carly demonstrates cognitive flexibility both in her ability to understand this alternative way of playing and in mentally switching back and forth between the roles. This is another significant leap forward in development of self-regulation.

> After about 5 minutes, Chloe says that the baby's bottle is empty and they need to go to the store to buy some milk. Carly says that she wants to be the "store lady."
> The other children agree and all three children now become involved in rearranging the play space and gathering props to play store.

When children engage in cooperative play, they talk with one another before the play begins to plan what form the play will take and what role each child will play. They utilize their working memory to mentally keep track of a complex set of roles and rules. They must monitor their own behavior to stay in role, inhibit behaviors that do not follow the plan, and at the same time shift focus as their imaginary situation evolves. Their theme and their roles may shift several times over the course of the 30 minutes or so that they play together, as one or more of the children become interested in pursuing other ideas.

Play and Cognitive Flexibility

As these children get a bit older and their working memory becomes stronger, they will become less tolerant of departures from agreed-upon play themes and roles. Their inner ideas of what the play should look like become more precise and advanced, and thus they are more attuned to "errors" the other children make in playing out the pretend theme (even when they don't see their own errors). They freely attempt to regulate other children and, for the most part, allow themselves to be regulated by the group.

Chloe, now age 5, is in the middle of her kindergarten year at a private school. Next year she will join her brother at public school and attend aftercare at school until one of her parents picks her up in the evening. This year, however, she is picked up after school by a neighbor, a stay-at-home mom. Chloe and the neighbor's two sons—6-year-old Casey and 7-year-old Ian—play together at the neighbor's home for 2 hours after school. For 2 days, the children have been turning the neighbor's playroom into a "pirate hideout."

There have been intense—and sometimes argumentative—negotiations over ideas: who they are hiding from, what should be included in a hideout, and what kind of snacks pirates should eat. Yesterday, Chloe and her friends decided to have their afternoon snack in their hideout and to dress for the occasion. The mother helped them decide what kinds of snacks pirates might have available in their hideouts. When Chloe wanted to put on her princess dress for snack time, her playmates objected: They had just agreed that they would all be pirates. The boys vigorously disagreed with Chloe's suggestion that they change the play. In the end, she took off the princess costume and happily put on an eye patch.

Precisely because of their stronger working memory, they are much less likely to tolerate a group member who wants to veer off into a different type of play. However, even children who have difficulty regulating their behavior in response to directions from adults may be able to respond to feedback from their peer group, because the play activity is so enjoyable and they are highly motivated to continue it. This stricter regulation allows greater creativity to take place.

> Today they continue their pirate play with a discussion about whether one of them will be a bad pirate. They all want to be good pirates and turn their attention to setting up a safe place. "Let's pretend that there is a cave over here where we sleep." "Let's pretend that we have a fire right here." "Lets pretend we have guns." "Let's pretend that we have bows and arrows." "No, we're pirates, not Indians."

Even more than the 4-year-olds playing house, this play activity challenges the children's ability to regulate their behavior in keeping with internal ideas. The pirate play is less imitative of real-life situations than playing house. Here the children's thoughts are clearly mental tools that allow them to plan and imagine something that they have never experienced in real life—an exotic place called a pirate hideout. Also, while the 4-year-olds may have played house for 20 or 30 minutes, the pirate activity has taken place over 2 days and places strong demands on their working memory and ability to make and adhere to a plan.

> The children decide that some bad pirates are causing trouble for them, sneaking in at night and taking things that belong to them. "Let's pretend that we buried some treasure

here," says Chloe, indicating the underside of a pillow, "and when we wake up it's gone. The bad pirates took it." "We have to find them," says Casey. Chloe places her hands in front of one eye as if she is holding a telescope. "I see one," she says, pointing across the room. Casey aims an imaginary gun and shoots. "You missed him," says Ian. "I did not!" says Casey. "Well, I still see one," says Ian, as he takes aim with his own imaginary gun. "Maybe it's a different one."

As Ian shoots a second imaginary bad guy, Chloe warns, "I think there's a whole bunch of them." The three children then begin to make a plan for dealing with a whole bunch of bad guys.

They agree on these aspects of their play without actually setting something up physically. There are no props to represent the cave, the fire, or the guns. In this way, their play is more mature than when Chloe played house at age 4. The 4-year-olds relied on props to represent reality (checkers for food and money). Their actions were still linked to the objects, even though the actual objects were subordinate to the subjective reality that the children assigned to them. In the development of thought, this shows a transitional stage between the "purely physical constraints of early childhood and adult thought, which can be totally free of real situations" (Vygotsky, 1978, p. 98). In the pirate play of the older children, we can see that their play—and their thought—is becoming more internalized and more emancipated from situational constraints.

Barkley described reconstitution as "goal-directed behavioral flexibility and creativity" (1997, p. 188). We can clearly see this executive function in its overt, shared form as the three children plan and create the pirate hideout. As they discuss, argue, and negotiate how to play, they are mentally trying out different behavioral sequences before finally selecting one to act upon. According to Barkley, it is the internalization of the play function that later allows us to engage in cognitive flexibility. In its mature, covert, and internalized form, cognitive flexibility allows the individual to consider "multiple responses for the resolution of a problem or the attainment of a future goal" (Barkley, 1997, p. 188). This is essential to self-regulation.

Play and Development

Over the years, we can see that Chloe's play gradually relies more and more on internalized mental processes. As an infant and young toddler, she plays with blocks and other toys, experimenting with their physical properties and possible uses. As an older toddler, she learns to also play with ideas, as when she acts as if her block is a phone. As a preschooler, she becomes more adept at playing with internal ideas as she and her classmates experiment with themes and roles. As a kindergartner, she engages in complex manipulation of internal information, as she and her neighbors verbally negotiate and mentally audition complex ideas before activating them.

While many adults see children's play as simply a pleasant pastime (and some even view it as a waste of time), play activities can help children develop exactly the skills that they will need to succeed in school. As seen in these examples of Chloe's play life, as children mature their play activities also evolve, presenting age-appropriate opportunities to develop their executive functions. Chloe's play activities are voluntary, self-initiated, and self-directed. Although there is no "lesson plan" and no adult-initiated reward or punishment, her play activities are perfectly suited to help her progress from external regulation to internal regulation.

Self-Regulation as Instinct

Both Barkley and Vygotsky have theorized that all children follow a natural developmental path from externally to internally directed behavior. We have seen how both language and play, two central activities of childhood, begin in external form and are gradually internalized, providing the child with increased ability to regulate her own thoughts, perceptions, and emotions.

Barkley believes that children have an "instinct" or natural drive toward greater inner regulation. "The capacity for self-regulation is not taught but emerges as a result of an interaction between the child's maturing neurological capabilities for self-regulation (the executive functions) and his or her interactions with a social environment that stimulates, encourages, and places a premium on such behavior" (Barkley, 1997, p. 227). Barkley emphasizes the neurological and genetic basis of these processes. He stresses that both language and play—and the self-regulation they foster—develop as a result of the maturation of the prefrontal cortex. The social context, although important to the unfolding of the executive functions, "does not account for their existence" (Barkley, 1997, p. 234).

Vygotsky certainly agreed with this concept of an innate drive toward self-regulation, but he also devoted much attention to the social context in which that unfolding takes place. In other words, while acknowledging the central role of nature, he was also keenly aware of the role of nurture. In Chapter 5 we look more closely at Vygotsky's ideas about how social interactions, by eliciting and encouraging the child's self-regulatory capabilities, facilitate the development of executive function.

CHAPTER FIVE

Nature and Nurture

Understanding the Zone
of Proximal Development

ONE OF VYGOTSKY'S MOST important contributions to our understanding of the development of executive function is his emphasis on the dynamic relationship between internal and external aspects of development. His theory cautions us against viewing a child's capabilities as being only biologically determined and widens our perspective to include the social aspects of the developmental process. Vygotsky believed that higher mental functions are in part "socially formed and culturally determined" and that if one changes the mental tools available to a child, one can change the structure of the child's mind (Vygotsky, 1978, p. 126). Modern neuropsychological research lends credence to Vygotsky's theory, showing a remarkable plasticity in the development of the brain. "The same neuroplasticity that leaves executive functioning skills vulnerable to genetic and environmental disruption also presents the possibility of actively promoting the successful development of these skills" (Center on the Developing Child, 2011, p. 8).

Vygotsky's concept of the child's zone of proximal development (ZPD) helps us understand this dynamic relationship between inner and outer aspects of development.

ZPD and the Level of Assisted Performance

Vygotsky (1978) used the concept of ZPD to refer to a range of skills and higher mental functions that children do not consistently perform on their own, but that they can perform when given the right kind of assistance. For example, 2-year-old Chloe (Chapter 4) wants to put on her own socks. She tries but is unable to perform this task independently. Her mother recognizes that Chloe is partially capable and gives her just the right amount of support that she needs to get the job done.

According to Vygotsky, the development of any new skill or function occurs within the boundaries of the ZPD (see Figure 5.1). A great many skills are outside of the developmental competencies of the learner and thus inaccessible for the time being. At the same time, the child does reliably exhibit many skills on her own—her level of independent performance. There is also a slight overlap between the two, where we can observe those skills that the child cannot reliably exhibit on her own but—because there is enough underlying developmental competence—can perform with assistance. These competencies compose the ZPD: emerging abilities that will eventually become part of the child's level of independent performance. Between independent performance and maximally assisted performance lie varying degrees of partially assisted performance (Bodrova & Leong, 2007).

If we list the self-care tasks that Chloe could perform independently as a toddler, putting on her own socks would not be on the list. However, this skill is in her ZPD, because she

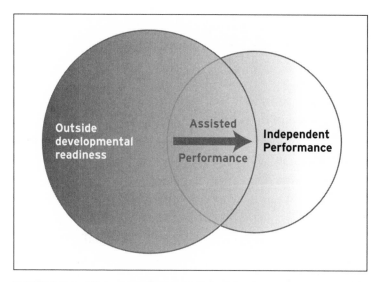

FIGURE 5.1. The zone of proximal development.

is developmentally ready to perform this task and is able to perform it with external support. If we view executive function development as a progression from externalized to internalized knowledge and actions, then the ZPD refers to the knowledge and actions that are still external and have not yet been internalized.

Shared Activities

Vygotsky differentiated between learning and development. He believed that the two processes are not identical but are united. According to his theory, properly organized learning "sets in motion developmental processes that would be impossible without learning" (Vygotsky, 1978, p. 90). Because learning takes place in a social context, understanding how that context affects learning, and thus development, can give us a road map for facilitating development of executive functions.

According to Vygotskian theory, the higher mental functions initially exist in their external form as shared activity between two or more people before they become internalized by the child (Bodrova & Leong, 2007). For example, when Chloe's mother helps her learn a strategy for putting on her socks, it is a shared activity that leads Chloe's development. As noted in Chapter 4, Chloe was not only learning how to put on her socks, she was also learning that language can provide strategies for solving problems.

It is not just adults who can promote a child's executive function through shared activity. Interaction with peers, especially in the context of play, also functions as a shared activity that provides external support for emerging functions.

On a Saturday afternoon, 5-year-old Chloe accompanies her father to her brother's ball game. Watching the game holds little interest for her; she would prefer to join the children at a playground on the other side of the field. Her father promises to take her there "after a while." He first tries to interest her in the game, and then tries to coax her into drawing with the markers and pad of paper that she brought along. But Chloe is restless and keeps interrupting his attention to the game. She repeatedly drops her markers under the bleachers and climbs down to get them, then climbs back up. During one trip under the bleachers, she wanders toward the playground until her father notices and calls her back. He takes the markers away from her and sternly tells her to remain in the bleachers and sit still. Chloe begins to whine and lies down on the floorboard of the bleachers. They are both relieved when her father's friend arrives with his own two daughters, 8-year-old Sasha and 9-year-old Rita. The two older girls invite Chloe to play with them and recruit other children for a game of Red Light, Green Light.

Vygotsky (1978) believed that play is a "leading activity" in the lives of preschoolers, meaning that play can provide a context for learning that leads development. For example, in Chloe's pretend play with peers (Chapter 4), the children foster one another's development by monitoring their own actions and those of their playmates to make sure that everyone is staying in role and on task. The monitoring facilitates the development of their working memory as they keep the respective roles in mind and on their response inhibition as they inhibit impulses to play in ways that are not in keeping with the current theme and roles.

The development of working memory and response inhibition is even more apparent in traditional games of older children such as Red Light, Green Light, which Sasha and Rita initiate (see Table 5.1).

Establishing a rectangular playing field the length of the bleachers, the children line up across the width of the field—the start line. Rita appoints herself leader (the red light). Chloe is unfamiliar with the game, and they explain the rules to her. Rita will move to the opposite end of the field, where she will turn her back on the rest of the group while saying "Green light, green light, green light." The other children can move toward her, but when she suddenly says "Red light" and twirls to face the group, the other children must freeze where they are. If the leader spies players making the slightest movement, they will be sent back to the start line. Everyone else has to hold their position—without

TABLE 5.1. Traditional Childhood Games and Executive Function

Game	Executive Function Required
Mother May I?	1. Response inhibition (inhibiting the prepotent response) The natural (prepotent) response is to respond to the direction to move forward. ("Take one giant step.") Players must inhibit this response until given the proper verbal cue. ("Yes you may.") 2. Working memory Players must remember to ask, "Mother, may I?" prior to taking any action. Players must also continually update working memory, discarding all instructions followed by the cue, "No, you may not" and retaining and responding to instructions given just prior to the cue, "Yes, you may."
Red Light, Green Light	1. Response inhibition (interrupting an ongoing response) Players initiate a response (moving forward) when given the verbal cue "Green light." They must immediately and completely stop that ongoing action when given the cue "Red light."
Statues	1. Response inhibition (interrupting an ongoing response) Following a period of ongoing free movement after they are swung around by the leader, players must completely stop this ongoing response (become statues).

TABLE 5.1. Continued

Game	Executive Function Required
	2. Response Inhibition (protecting the period of delay) Then players must continue to inhibit all action (including speech) for an extended period of time. Each player in turn must initiate action in response to a tactile cue (meaning that statue is "turned on") and again inhibit all responses in response to another tactile cue (that statue is "turned off"). They must ignore all other stimuli while in the off position, including comments by the leader, actions of other statues, and internal discomforts such as itches, tired muscles, and so on.
Freeze Tag	1. Response inhibition (interrupting an ongoing response) Players must stop all movement in response to a tactile cue (being tagged by the player who is It) and continue to inhibit all movement until they receive another tactile cue (being tagged by another player).
Simon Says	1. Working memory Players must remember to respond only to instructions preceded by the cue "Simon says." They must discard all other instructions from their working memory and retain and respond only to the properly cued instructions.

(*continued*)

TABLE 5.1. Continued

Game	*Executive Function Required*
	2. Response inhibition (inhibiting the prepotent response) Players must inhibit the natural tendency to respond to the various commands ("Jump up and down"; "Stick out your tongue") and respond only when the command is preceded by the correct verbal cue ("Simon says stick out your tongue"). The leader deliberately tries to trick the players into responding too soon.

Many traditional childhood games tap the executive functions of working memory and response inhibition. Some researchers see working memory and inhibition control as practically inseparable constructs that form the core of executive function. These games are an example of how peer-initiated, shared activities can lead to development of executive function.

any movement—until Rita turns her back again and says, "Green light." The first child to make it all the way to the other side of the field will become the new red light and the game will start again.

When Chloe engaged in dramatic play with her peers, the pretend theme was the primary motivating factor, and monitoring and regulating herself and others was secondary, a means to keep the dramatic play focused and on track. In games such as Red Light, Green Light, monitoring and regulation become the primary purpose of the game. The pretend aspect of this game is minimal: there is no actual red light, no props of any kind. The external trappings of play are no longer as important; what matters is the internal abilities of the players.

As the youngest child in the group, Chloe is often sent back to the start line when she fails to stop moving quickly enough or when she is unable to hold her frozen position. But she persists in the activity, improves her performance, and much prefers playing this game to watching her brother's ball game or coloring in the bleachers.

The Future Child

We can see that Chloe functions on a higher level when she leaves her father's side at the ball game and joins the older children to play Red Light, Green Light. On the bleachers watching the game with her father, her level of self-regulation is that of a typical 5-year-old: She is restless, talkative, and climbs all over the bleachers. Moments later, the interaction with the other children in the context of the game provides her a system of external support that allows her to exhibit an exemplary level of self-regulation. It is as though we are seeing two different girls. On the bleachers, her behavioral control is just average, while in the context of the game we see a much higher level of behavioral control. Chloe's eagerness to improve her performance allows us to see what lies ahead for her. The behavioral monitoring in this game is within Chloe's ZPD and will, in the future, be internalized. She will be capable of conducting behavioral self-monitoring in a variety of nonplay situations.

It is within the ZPD that others have the opportunity to interact with that "future child," responding to skills and functions that have not yet matured but are emerging. When

Chloe is 14 months old and her brother builds a tower for her and tumbles it over, he notices her delight and eagerness to repeat the activity. She is far from being able to perform it independently; however, her brother intuitively understands that she will be able to do so in the near future, and he guides her play in that direction. In Vygotskian terms, he is interacting with the future child.

Experience of Empowerment

These interactions with the future child provide us a glimpse of what is to come and provide the child with an experience of empowerment. If we observe Chloe at age 2 when her mother helps her put on her socks, we can see from Chloe's interest, cooperation, and pleasure that this is a very different experience than having her mother put on her socks for her.

The experience provides Chloe with the opportunity to direct her own behavior and leaves her eager to continue to improve her performance. Chloe's reaction lets her mother know that her intervention was on the mark. She met Chloe at that spot within her ZPD where her abilities are emerging and her development is ready to be led.

Dynamics of the ZPD

Elena Bodrova and Deborah Leong are the developers of the Tools of the Mind curriculum, a Vygotsky-based approach to early childhood education. They and other students of Vygotsky have attempted to understand exactly how these shared activities promote development. They have identified several processes including *scaffolding, structuring or sequencing,* and *amplification* (Bodrova & Leong, 2007).

Scaffolding

The type of assistance that Chloe's mother provided in helping Chloe put on her socks is often referred to as scaffolding. With scaffolding, the task itself does not change over time, but the amount of external support does. Initially Chloe's actions are made easier with assistance. As Chloe becomes more knowledgeable and skilled, her mother gives less support and allows Chloe to do more of it herself. It may take Chloe multiple repetitions, and her mother may provide varying types (physical, verbal) and degrees of assistance, before Chloe masters the task and it becomes part of her level of independent performance.

At age 14 months, Chloe's level of independent performance consisted of putting the blocks into a container and dumping them out. But when her brother joined in her play, her level of assisted performance included using the blocks to first build a tower and then tumble it over. Initially, her only contribution was to tumble the tower after her brother built it. But he encouraged her to participate in building the tower, showing her how to stack one block on top of another. The building-and-tumbling game was within Chloe's zone of proximal development. Her brother provided less support as she became more capable. Here again, the task—building and tumbling a tower—did not change over time. What changed was that Chloe's actions became increasingly self-directed as she moved from assisted performance to independent performance.

Scaffolding need not be person to person, as in the above examples. It can also be provided by mediators. When Jon's therapist had him create a wrist list (Chapters 1 and 2), the list was a mediator providing the right amount of scaffolding for Jon to complete his chores. Mediators help children to perform independently in situations that otherwise would require more adult supervision (Bodrova & Leong, 2007). Another example of a mediator is the use of carpet squares during preschool circle time. When a child sits on the square it reminds him to stay seated within his personal space and not move around the room or touch other children. Mediators need not be physical. When children use counting rhymes ("One potato, two potato . . .) to decide who goes first, the rhyme is a mediator that helps the children settle or prevent disagreements without needing the intervention of an adult. As with person-to-person scaffolding, mediators can be phased out over time, as children become more capable of regulating their own behavior.

Structuring or Sequencing

Another way to provide assistance within the child's ZPD is through the process of sequencing, in which a new way of doing things is developed in incremental steps. For example, at 2 years of age, Chloe exhibits a new level of cognitive flexibility when she pretends that one of her blocks is a phone (Chapter 4). Her father notices this new development and first joins with her at that level: He picks up his phone and imitates her action. He then takes this pretend play to a slightly more complex level: He encourages Chloe to carry on a conversation with him while holding the "phone" to her ear. Once he sees that she is able to engage in that level of pretending, he takes it a step further and helps her to pretend that her mother, who is not present, is now on the phone. Chloe is able to pretend to speak to her mother; however, she is not able to pretend that her mother is talking with her. That level of imaginative play was not within her ZPD. She had reached the maximum level of assisted performance. Her father recognized this and did not press ahead any further.

In this case, Chloe's level of independent performance was to act as if the block were something else. By herself, she probably would not have gone beyond this level that day. But her father noted her interest in this new type of play. By offering a sequence of small steps beyond her level of independent performance, he engaged her at a level of assisted performance that held her interest and paved the way for additional gains.

Amplifying

Another concept that helps us understand the dynamics of the ZPD is the amplification of learning. Amplification stands in opposition to acceleration, which emphasizes moving children ahead in the developmental sequence, pushing them to independent performance (Bodrova & Leong, 2005). In contrast, amplification involves helping children to get the maximum benefit of their current ZPD before moving on. It recognizes that interaction in the ZPD provides rich opportunities which are developmentally appropriate and which lay a firm foundation for future development.

In Chloe's preschool activities, as well as in her afterschool play with neighbors, her teacher and the neighbor's mother provided the children with the opportunity to amplify the development of their executive function skills through participation in what Bodrova and Leong (2007) call "mature play." With its demands on her executive functions, Chloe's pretend play at ages 4 and 5 is substantively different than her earlier pretend play as a young toddler. For example, in her earlier play with her doll, Chloe reenacted behaviors that she had experienced her parents performing for her. She pushed the doll in its stroller, put it in its bed, and attempted to change its clothes. Her later play went far beyond reenactment of experiences. She called upon many inner resources and performed complex organization of her thoughts and behavior to engage in playing house as a 4-year-old and playing pirates as a 5-year-old.

The structure of Chloe's preschool program and her opportunity to engage in dramatic play at her neighbor's home provided both time and external support to plan and develop these complex themes. Not all children make the transition to playing at this more mature level. For many children, especially those who have come from disordered, chaotic environments, play may remain at the reenactment level and may not provide the opportunity to engage their working memory, response inhibition, cognitive flexibility, and planning abilities.

ZPD: A Framework for Planning Interventions That Facilitate Development

In the above examples, the scaffolding, sequencing, and amplifying are provided informally by Chloe's family, preschool teacher, and neighbor. For the most part, these interventions are spontaneous and intuitive and are not deliberately planned. However, Vygotsky's concept of a ZPD can also provide a framework for creating planned interventions that facilitate development.

The Role of the Facilitator

Participating in shared activities with a child is different from teaching. In our typical conception of the teacher-student relationship, the teacher's role is to decide what should be taught and to then impart that knowledge to the student, verbally or through demonstration. The student's role is first to listen or observe, then repeat the information or action. The teacher trains the student by praising desired behavior and correcting undesired behavior, perhaps using reward and punishment. It is a top-down model of development.

When Chloe's mother helps her learn to put on her socks, development begins from the bottom. Her mother notices Chloe's emerging interest and responds to it. Chloe's interest drives the development; she does not perform because of praise or criticism, reward, or punishment. She is internally motivated to learn and master the new behavior. Her mother's actions help her master this task more quickly than proceeding by imitation or trial and error. Her mother's actions can be likened to the role of facilitator rather than teacher. We borrow this concept from social learning theory and use it here to mean a person who:

1. Recognizes the child's developmental readiness to acquire a new skill or capacity
2. Intervenes in response to that readiness
3. Actively involves the child in the learning process
4. Evaluates the child's response, recognizing whether the intervention has provided an experience of empowerment that leaves the child motivated to learn more

Facilitating Executive Function Through Program Planning

These principles can be provided formally by educators who develop curricula that include executive function–facilitating activities. The Tools of the Mind curriculum, developed by Bodrova and Leong, is one such curriculum. In the Tools approach, the teacher purposefully facilitates executive functioning with procedures such as telling oneself out loud what one should do (using private speech), engaging in lots of dramatic play (structured so that planning is part of the play), and playing games similar to Simon Says and Red Light, Green Light to promote working memory, response inhibition, and cognitive flexibility (Bodrova & Leong, 2007). In 2007, research by Adele Diamond found that the Tools of the Mind curriculum improved executive functions for preschoolers in regular classrooms with regular teachers at minimal expense (Diamond, Barnett, Thomas, & Munro, 2007). In a 2011 article, Diamond and Lee reviewed new research that focuses on a diverse group of programs and activities that show promise for fostering development, including computer-based programs that improve working memory, athletic programs and martial arts that improve general functions, and classroom curricula similar to Tools of the Mind that provide comprehensive strategies that can be integrated into school programs.

We are encouraged by the current interest and research in the field of executive function, and we look forward to hearing about more schoolwide developments such as the Tools of the Mind. We hope to see the day when every child receives an education, from preschool through high school, that nurtures and supports the development of executive functions alongside academic knowledge and skills.

Facilitation for Individual Children

For now, however, the challenge of helping children with difficulties will fall on the shoulders of their parents along with the teachers, counselors, pediatricians, and other professionals involved in their lives. Those are the people who are in a position to recognize signs of difficulties and plan interventions to facilitate executive function development. In assessing difficulties and planning interventions, these adults act as facilitators.

Some children, like Chloe, enter school already well prepared to meet its demands. But not all children are so fortunate. Children come to school with huge differences in executive function. This is particularly evident in school settings because the school structure places strong demands—academically, behaviorally, and socially—on children's executive functioning. Children who are weak in any area of functioning can begin to fall behind their peers, and as they grow older these weaknesses become evident not only in the classroom but on the playground and at home as well. In the examples of Jon, Connor, Amanda, and Marcus in Chapter 3, we noted that each child depended on external support from others to regulate his or her behavior. While these four children are on the same developmental path as their peers, they are not as far along on that external-to-internal continuum.

Fortunately, the concept of ZPD—and its related concept of facilitating development—gives us a framework for planning interventions that can provide the right kinds of support for these children. Facilitators take a bottom-up approach, recognizing signs of the future child and building on those capabilities.

In the next chapter, we return to the story of Amanda (see Chapter 3) and see how her teacher performs the first steps in facilitation: recognizing and assessing Amanda's developmental needs and readiness.

CHAPTER SIX

Maintaining a Developmental Perspective

Dynamic Assessment of Executive Function

THE ZPD IS A fluid, ever-changing range of behaviors. As one behavior is mastered and becomes part of the child's level of independent performance, new expectations are introduced and new behaviors are able to be performed with assistance. The rate of progress through the ZPD varies from child to child. One child may need minimal help to move from assisted to independent performance. Another child may need much time and multiple types of support in multiple settings before a behavior reaches the level of independent performance.

Since the ZPD is fluid, it makes sense for our method of assessing children to be fluid as well. All too often, however, children's performance is assessed only in static terms, with a focus on what the child is able to do independently.

Traditional Assessment and Intervention

Four-year-old Amanda (Chapter 3) has great difficulty following classroom rules. At the beginning of the school year,

Ms. Blum tries various in-school techniques: redirection, reminders of the rules, praise for following the rules, and time outs for especially inappropriate behaviors. These interventions have limited success and, as a next step, Ms. Blum calls Amanda's parents in for a meeting. At the meeting, Ms. Blum provides an informal assessment of Amanda's progress in preschool. She is on target for all of her preacademic skills, but behaviorally she is immature. The most problematic behaviors are that Amanda is not keeping her hands to herself and is not following the teacher's directions.

This is a traditional way of assessing a child's behavioral maturity—with checklists and verbal descriptions of what the child can and cannot do. The target behaviors are reported in static black-and-white terms: She does this, she does not do that. In terms of ZPD, it is a statement of the child's level of independent performance.

Amanda's parents are pleased with the report of her academic readiness, but surprised and concerned by the problem behavior. They report that she usually listens to them fairly well. They admit, however, that since she is an only child, they have not placed many demands on her in daily life. They also tell Ms. Blum that Amanda spends most of her time around adults and older cousins, so they have not had much opportunity to observe how she acts with peers.

The parents are eager to follow any suggestions Ms. Blum might have for them. She sets up a system for sending home a daily report. Each day, Amanda will earn either a smiley face or a sad face for each of two behavioral expectations, depending on whether she has kept her hands to herself and followed teacher's instructions. With a sad face, Ms. Blum will add a note explaining the problem behavior. The parents' role will be to review the report daily, praise Amanda for a smiley face, talk with her about a sad face, and remind her of the importance of following the rules. Ms. Blum cautions the parents not to do any more than that. Specifically, she tells them not to punish Amanda at home if she earns a sad face, as the punishment would be too far removed in time from the offense to have any meaning for a 4-year-old.

Based on her assessment, Ms. Blum is setting up an intervention. The behavioral goal is also stated in terms of level of independent performance. Amanda will be praised and rewarded for bringing her behavior in line with the level of her classmates. There is also a tacit agreement between the teacher and the parents that, based on Amanda's academic readiness and the absence of problems at home, Amanda should be able to meet these behavioral expectations in the classroom. The underlying assumption here is that she only needs to be properly motivated to do so, and the praise from her parents along with the consequences already in place at school will provide that motivation. This assumption is not based on any specific data about Amanda's behavior (e.g., neither of them have observed occasions when Amanda improved the target behavior in response to praise or other consequences). Rather, it is assumed that children in general are motivated by praise and other consequences.

This daily report is implemented, and Amanda brings home sad faces on most days. Ms. Blum feels bad about sending so many sad faces, so looks for reasons to give her a smiley face. On those days, her parents praise her extravagantly and even give her special privileges: an extra treat after dinner or some money to spend at the store. They never punish her for bringing home a sad face, but they do talk with her daily about the behaviors noted on the reports ("Took Juan's paper away from him and threw it in the trash"; "Didn't listen when teacher said it was time to line up to go to the bathroom"; "Pushed LaShandra down on the playground").

At first, Amanda's parents ask her why she behaved in that way and they explain to her why the behavior was wrong. During these discussions they are somewhat surprised to encounter an argumentative and bossy side of Amanda that they had not noticed before. They promise her larger rewards if she will bring home more smiley faces. But the pattern of primarily sad-faced reports continues. Now Amanda begins to whine or cry when they talk to her about her day. Her parents shorten the discussion and just give her a quick talk about why she shouldn't act that way.

The daily report does not yield any improvement. However, neither the teacher nor the parents question (1) the goal being set at the level of independent performance or (2) the underlying assumption that the solution to the problem lies in motivating Amanda through praise and other consequences. In spite of the lack of progress, they continue with the same intervention, perhaps hoping that it will suddenly begin to work or that Amanda will outgrow the behavior.

Dynamic Assessment

In early October, Ms. Blum has to take an extended maternity leave, and Ms. LeBlanc takes over the class. She has observed the class in action and she knows the history of interventions attempting to bring Amanda's behavior in line with classroom expectations. The daily report is still in place.

She decides to do her own assessment of Amanda's behavior.

> Ms. LeBlanc calls Amanda's mother and lets her know that she will discontinue the daily report until she gets to know Amanda better. Amanda's mother expresses relief; she tells Ms. LeBlanc that the daily review of the report has become something that she dreads. It is also causing problems between her and her husband, who is angry that Amanda is not improving and thinks that they should punish Amanda for the continued misbehavior.

The daily report is a constant reminder to the parents that their daughter is not meeting the behavioral expectations of her classroom. Although Ms. Blum had cautioned the parents not to punish Amanda at home for behavior at school, the assumption that Amanda just needs to be motivated causes the parents to view her behavior as willful noncompliance, since they have done their best to motivate her.

> In the classroom, Ms. LeBlanc introduces a new game at circle time that she calls Stop and Go. The children first stand and face their teacher. When she begins playing music softly in the background, the children move to the music. Their feet must remain in place and their eyes must remain on the teacher, but they are free to move the rest of their bodies in any way that the music inspires them. Ms. LeBlanc moves along with them, but she only moves one hand, as the other hand is hidden behind her back. Suddenly she calls out "Stop!" and brings a bright red stop sign from behind her back. The children freeze where they are. Ms. LeBlanc walks among them and comments on all of the interesting "stat-

ues" in the classroom. The children remain frozen until Ms. LeBlanc says "Go!" and returns the stop sign to its hiding place behind her back. The children move for another minute, when the music ends, the stop sign is put away, and the children sit down for a story.

As Ms. LeBlanc leads the Stop and Go game, she is particularly interested in observing Amanda. At the end of the week, she notes that, during the few minutes of the games each day, Amanda has been not only able but eager to show good self-control. Ms. LeBlanc makes a mental note to discuss this with Amanda's parents.

After 2 weeks, Ms. LeBlanc calls the parents and sets up a meeting. She shares observations similar to Ms. Blum's: Amanda shows good academic performance but poor behavioral performance, the most problematic being physical interference with the other children and not following instructions. Those behaviors cause the most disruption in the classroom and often cause Amanda to be ostracized by the other children.

Ms. LeBlanc also notes, however, that there are a few occasions when Amanda does keep her hands to herself and does follow instructions. There is one girl in the class, Celia, whom Amanda seems to look up to. She is never bossy with Celia as she is with the other children and never tries to physically intervene in what Celia is doing. Ms. LeBlanc has also noticed that Amanda follows instructions exceptionally well, from both herself and the assistant teacher, but only when no other children are nearby. Her impression is that when other children are around, Amanda is too busy reacting to their behavior to respond to the teacher's instructions. Finally, Ms. LeBlanc tells the parents that in spite of Amanda's apparent difficulty with impulse control, she does very well at the Stop and Go game. She keeps her eyes on her teacher and is able to stop on cue and to stay frozen until she receives the cue to go.

Amanda is not behaving any differently for Ms. LeBlanc than she did for Ms. Blum. If Ms. LeBlanc had continued sending home a daily report, she too would have been hard pressed to find a day that would rate a smiley face for either behavior. However, Ms. LeBlanc is assessing Amanda's behavior in a different way. In contrast to Ms. Blum's assessment of Amanda's behaviors in static terms, this assessment emphasizes that the behaviors change depending on the context in which they occur. Ms. LeBlanc is able to provide the parents with data about when and where Amanda is able to meet expectations.

> Ms. LeBlanc tells the parents that she will do some things differently at school to help Amanda. She will seat Amanda near Celia more often and observe their interaction. Also, based on her impression that Amanda is too preoccupied with other children to listen closely to directions, Ms. LeBlanc will make it a point, as often as possible, to get good eye contact with her before beginning instructions and see if that will help Amanda stay focused on their conversation.
>
> The parents tell Ms. LeBlanc that, now that they are more aware of the problems at school, they have noticed similar behaviors at home. Amanda is bossy with some of her older cousins, and although the other children laugh about it and usually give in to her, she does get very angry and even physical if they do not. Ms. LeBlanc suggests that the parents could invite children from school over for play dates to give Amanda a chance to get to know them better and also

to give the parents a chance to view their daughter's interaction with peers.

Ms. LeBlanc decides not to resume the daily written report. Instead she will send them e-mail updates and let them know the results of her plan to pair Amanda and Celia more often and to get direct eye contact before giving instructions. If these interventions don't help, she will try something else.

In Vygotskian terms, the process that Ms. LeBlanc has initiated would be called a dynamic assessment. It includes not just Amanda's level of independent performance, but her level of assisted performance. Whereas the previous assessment led to just one type of intervention (administering positive and negative consequences), this assessment highlights several interventions that might be helpful in eliciting and supporting the desired behaviors. In other words, Ms. LeBlanc is looking for ways to scaffold the desired behaviors. The next day, Ms. LeBlanc has an opportunity to involve Amanda in some play with Celia.

During center time, Celia, Drew, and Emma have decided to play house. Ms. LeBlanc notices that Amanda is watching their play. Interested in observing whether Amanda can enter this unstructured play, she asks Amanda if she would like to play house with them. Amanda nods, keeping her eyes on the other children. Ms. LeBlanc brings Amanda into the housekeeping center and the other children willingly accept her into the group. Ms. LeBlanc steps aside and observes as the children assign roles. Emma says that she wants to be the mother and Drew agrees with Celia's suggestion that he be the father.

To Ms. LeBlanc's surprise, Amanda states that she wants to be a baby. The other children agree, and Celia volunteers to be the big sister. Amanda is instructed to sit on the floor. When she does, Celia gives her a cup which she says is a sippy cup. Amanda pretends to drink from the cup, while the other children set the dishes on the table and pretend to cook food on the stove. When Amanda makes a suggestion about the meal, Celia says that the baby should only talk baby talk. Amanda not only complies with this directive, she remains seated on the floor. Celia pats her on the head and says, "Good baby." Amanda smiles and responds with baby talk.

When Amanda joins her classmates who are playing house and takes on the role of the baby, she has sufficient self-control to fulfill the group's expectations for that role, which call for her to be docile and cooperative. In this pretend play, her teacher is able to get a glimpse of the "future Amanda," a child who is able to regulate her behavior in keeping with classroom expectations.

When Ms. LeBlanc checks back on them 10 minutes later, the children are reorganizing the play. They now have a play dog, and Drew says that it has a broken leg. At Drew's suggestion, the children decide that Drew should now be the "animal doctor." Celia and Emma switch roles as big sister and mother. Amanda once again says that she wants to be the baby. Celia and Emma decide that Amanda will be allowed to walk now, but she must hold the big sister's hand. The play dishes are cleared from the table, which becomes the doctor's examining table. They all maintain their assigned roles, including Amanda, who docilely holds Emma's hand, uses baby talk, and follows the lead of the other three children.

Ms. LeBlanc again is amazed that Amanda, usually very domineering with the other children, has not only asked to play a passive and dependent role, but has managed to exhibit those behaviors consistently for over 10 minutes. She is not sure what all this means, but she mentally files this new information to reflect on later.

Ms. LeBlanc is performing an in-depth—and time-consuming—assessment by gathering information from a variety of contexts that give her a more nuanced understanding of Amanda's ability to regulate her behavior. With that information, she will be in a position to plan more effective interventions.

One afternoon when Amanda's mother comes to pick her up, Ms. LeBlanc invites her to stay and talk. She shares her new observations, in particular how well Amanda played with the other children in the housekeeping center. Amanda's mother says that she has not had a chance to set up any play dates. However, last weekend she invited some of Amanda's cousins over for a visit, and she asked the older children not to give in when Amanda was bossy with them. They all played a board game, and when Amanda insisted on winning, her mother intervened and said that if Amanda didn't play fair, her cousins would have to go home. Amanda calmed down and finished the game.

Dynamic Assessment and the Future Child

Every classroom is likely to have at least one child like Amanda, a child with satisfactory academic skills but poor executive function. Dynamic assessment is particularly helpful for these children. It allows us to see beyond a child's actual (independent) level of performance and get a glimpse of the child's potential functioning—the future child. This is actually assessment and intervention at once: It shows us what the child is capable of and also encourages us to look for ways to bring that potential performance to fruition.

The goal of dynamic assessment is to help the facilitator ascertain what kinds of support will allow her to connect with the child at his current level and move him along to the next level of development. We conclude this chapter with a summary of how Ms. LeBlanc conducted her dynamic assessment and how it gave both Ms. LeBlanc and Amanda's parents a glimpse of the future child.

1. Ms. LeBlanc went beyond a static description of Amanda's level of independent functioning. Because of the fluid nature of the ZPD, there is almost always some aspect of the targeted ability that the child can demonstrate with the right kind of external support. Ms. LeBlanc sought to determine Amanda's level of assisted development.

2. Ms. LeBlanc didn't think only about Amanda's behavior but about contexts. To explore the full range of Amanda's potential, she considered Amanda's functioning in as many different contexts as possible. For example, she noted that Amanda was able to keep her hands to herself around Celia and to follow teacher instructions quite well when no other children were around. Such situations yield important information about what kinds of external support may be helpful in other contexts. Ms. LeBlanc also gathered information regarding contexts outside school. For example, through her conversations with Amanda's parents, Ms. LeBlanc learned that Amanda was able to shift

focus and regulate her emotions and behavior while playing a board game at home with her older cousins, motivated by her desire to continue playing with them.

3. Ms. LeBlanc intentionally created new contexts that might reveal higher levels of functioning for Amanda. For example, Ms. LeBlanc introduced the Stop and Go game as a means of evaluating Amanda's response inhibition. She also arranged for Amanda to be included in group play with Celia and two other children and observed the dynamics of Amada's self-control and cognitive flexibility in that context.

4. In creating these new contexts, Ms. LeBlanc included play. As Vygotsky noted, play gives us an opportunity to view the future child. These play interventions yielded information about Amanda's potential that could not obtained only during circle time or art projects.

5. Ms. LeBlanc made note of Amanda's responsiveness to interventions and didn't look just for fully developed behaviors but for partially developed, or emerging, behaviors. The previous assessment had targeted and evaluated only one level: the expectation that Amanda would keep her hands to herself and follow the teacher's instructions for a full day. Ms. LeBlanc's assessment targeted much more modest behavioral expectations, for example, the ability to interrupt her activity in response to a cue by the teacher. Ms. LeBlanc recognized that self-regulation is a gradual process and that development occurs in small sequences.

6. Ms. LeBlanc shared information with Amanda's parents in a way that encouraged them to engage fully in the assessment process. As Ms. LeBlanc updated her understanding of Amanda's performance in various contexts, she passed that information along to the parents. This in turn encouraged the parents to look at how Amanda functioned in

other contexts (at home, with cousins) and to share that information with Ms. LeBlanc. This gave both parties a fuller understanding of Amanda's emerging abilities.

7. Ms. LeBlanc treated assessment as an ongoing process, with evaluation and intervention closely entwined, rather than two separate processes. Interventions that are tried out as part of the assessment can, when successful, inspire more interventions. (In Part III, we will see how Ms. Le-Blanc uses an expansion of the Stop and Go game to help Amanda have more self-control in ordinary classroom situations.)

PART III

Interventions That Support Executive Function

CHAPTER SEVEN

The Mental Health Professional as Facilitator

Planning Interventions That Support Emerging Executive Functions

CHILDREN EXPERIENCE DELAYS IN the development of executive function for a variety of reasons. Genetically based conditions such as ADHD, autism spectrum disorders, learning disabilities, and anxiety disorders are known to be associated with delays or disruptions. But environmental factors such as neglect and trauma can also disrupt the development of executive function. According to the Center on the Developing Child at Harvard University, these adverse environments can impair the development of executive functions due to "disruptive effects of toxic stress on the developing architecture of the brain" (2011, p. 7). The center expresses grave concern that the mislabeling of these problems can lead to expulsion from the classroom or inappropriate use of medication rather than to developmentally sensitive support for emerging functions.

Mental health clinicians are in a unique position to help parents and teachers recognize signs of difficulty. A child with any of the above-mentioned conditions is likely to come to the attention of a mental health professional at some point. Whether or not the child's presenting symptoms are couched in executive function terminology, a majority of children referred for mental health services will have problems in self-regulation. Some of the ways that the clinician can be involved in developmentally sensitive assessment and intervention include the following:

1. Introduce a dynamic assessment process and set goals for intervention.
2. Identify persons who can act as facilitators and engage them in that role.
3. Engage the child's interest by introducing developmentally appropriate interventions.
4. Plan external support (scaffolding) for guiding development at the point of performance.
5. Sequence and amplify the interventions, adjusting the level of support in response to the child's level of performance.
6. Introduce a long-term vision, engaging the child as an active partner in treatment and engaging other facilitators as partners in ongoing dynamic assessment.

In the following four chapters, we take up the stories of the children (Amanda, Marcus, Connor, and Jon) presented in Chapter 3. We look at ways that mental health clinicians, along with the children's parents and teachers, responded to the children's difficulties by planning developmentally sensitive interventions that supported their emerging executive functions. In this chapter, we first preview the role of clinicians in these case examples.

Introducing a Dynamic Assessment

A dynamic assessment reframes the problem, using the concept of executive function, and thus gives the parents and teachers a new lens for viewing the child and for setting realistic goals. What was formerly seen as laziness or willful disobedience can be understood in terms of specific brain functions that need additional time to develop and, in the meantime, require more external support. Beginning with the presenting problems, the clinician gathers information from parents and teachers, keeping the ZPD in mind. The purpose of the dynamic assessment is to discover specific demonstrations of what the child can do with the assistance of others (level of assisted performance) and therefore has the potential to develop more fully.

Identifying Facilitators

When children have problems in self-regulation, parents typically view their duties in terms of discipline. By the time they come to the clinician, they have usually tried using praise or reward and criticism or punishment to influence and shape their child's behavior, based on the assumption that the child needs motivation. Many parents will say that they have tried everything, and this is often true. The parents may have other children, and applying positive and negative consequences with those children works. The children change their behavior to obtain the positive consequences and to avoid the negative consequences. The parents are truly at a loss to understand why these methods don't work with the child that they have brought in for treatment and often have no idea what to do next.

When the clinician reframes the problem as a difficulty with executive functions, this often relieves tension that has built up in the relationship between parents and child. The next step is for the clinician to explain the role of a facilitator.

It can be compared to the process of teaching the child to ride a bike. Most parents intuitively understand the scaffolding that a child needs to learn to ride a bike. And they understand that the learning process varies widely from child to child: Some take to it right away and need little help, while others may need much more adult support before they can ride independently. But in the end, both kinds of learners are able to ride and enjoy it just as much. This analogy helps parents understand that their "problem child" just needs more developmental readiness and more external support. They can then intuitively see why their previous methods haven't worked. You don't teach a child to ride a bike by telling him he just needs to try harder, or that he just needs to use his sense of balance. Offering rewards or threatening punishment is not going to change the outcome for a child who is not developmentally ready to ride a bike.

Planning Developmentally Appropriate Interventions

A playful activity is often the best way to introduce the child to an executive function–related concept. For example, in Chapter 2, Jon's therapist used a game (Ready, Set, Go for It!, Activity 2.1) to introduce him to the concept of working memory. Because Jon was physically, mentally, and emotionally involved in the game, the lesson had a much greater impact than if they had just sat and talked about the concept of working memory. Once the child's interest is engaged, the therapist can then link the concept to real life, showing the child how the ability that he has just demonstrated in the game is essential in everyday situations. By linking the executive function to situations that are important to the child, the therapist increases the child's motivation to participate in therapy and follow through on assignments.

Providing External Support at the Point of Performance

Explaining executive function to a child and giving the child the opportunity to practice related behaviors through games and activities is only the beginning. Understanding does not mean that the child will be able to reliably perform the behavior in the day-to-day flow of activities. For the child to function on a level playing field with peers, external support needs to be in place at the point of performance.

The clinician plans ways to provide scaffolding that compensates for the child's specific deficits. During scaffolding the child can function at his or her potential rather than actual level of development. The behavioral expectation does not change, but the child is given sufficient external support to meet the expectation. Often this means that the clinician devises a plan by which a caregiver can give the child the "just right" amount of support when the behavior is expected.

Another way of providing scaffolding is to use a mediator, which is a tool the child can use that will help to facilitate the desired level of performance. It can provide an intermediary kind of scaffolding between full external support and independent performance. When Jon used a wrist list to support his working memory, it helped him complete his chores without relying on his mother for reminders. In Chapter 9, a particular mediator is used in a variety of situations to support Marcus's weak goal orientation.

Scaffolding, whether personal or via mediation, is left in place until the child shows mastery and is able to perform independently. As the child improves, some of the assistance is removed. If the improvement continues, other support can be gradually removed until the child performs independently. Sometimes scaffolding may be needed indefinitely; in which case the child may learn to provide his or her own scaffolding.

Adjusting Support According to Performance

The clinician sequences interventions by beginning with less challenging contexts and moving to more challenging contexts as the child performs more reliably. For example, interventions might begin at home, giving the child the opportunity to master a skill there before demonstrating it in school or in social situations. The clinician may also amplify interventions by providing opportunities for the child to practice the skill in multiple contexts. Once the child shows mastery, the amount of support can be scaled back.

In Chapter 6, Ms. LeBlanc introduced a game called Stop and Go to assess Amanda's ability to regulate her behavior. In Chapter 8, we will see how Ms. LeBlanc sequentially adjusts the game to provide support for Amanda in more challenging situations. Then, as Amanda responds to that support, Ms. LeBlanc is able to gradually scale back the amount of direct support that she gives.

Introducing a Long-Term Vision

Sometimes a child's difficulties with executive function will continue for the long term. Thus, although the child's performance improves, the child may need continued support to keep up with peers as they forge ahead with their own development.

One of the clinician's long-term goals should be to encourage the parents and other caregivers to understand the ZPD as a lens for viewing their child's ongoing needs. As one competency is mastered, others are emerging, and caregivers will need to continue to find the right amount of support to facilitate optimum development.

Also, it is equally important to help older children to "own" the problem and become active participants in managing their difficulties. Treatment will be most effective when children view themselves as active partners rather than viewing treatment as something done to or for them by adults. According to Bodrova and Leong, the role of the facilitator is to arm children with mental tools. That means that the facilitator goes beyond the goal of improving performance; the long-term goal is to enable the child to use tools independently and creatively and to "provide a path to independence" (Bodrova & Leong, 2007, p. 4).

Overview of Case Examples

In the next four chapters, we return to the case examples presented in Chapter 3 and describe the clinician's role and the interventions used in each case. The cases are presented chronologically, beginning with the youngest child, Amanda (age 4), and ending with Jon (age 10). The older the child, the greater his or her involvement in planning and implementing the interventions (see below). While each case highlights a particular executive function, in reality multiple functions are always involved in treatment.

Chapter 8: Amanda, Age 4, Preschool

Clinician's role: The clinician is involved as a monthly consultant to the preschool that Amanda attends. The clinician works with Amanda's teacher to design classroom-based interventions that support Amanda in shifting focus.

Child's role: Amanda is not directly involved in setting goals or planning interventions.

Chapter 9: Marcus, Age 7, Second Grade

Clinician's role: The clinician becomes involved when, upon advice from Marcus's pediatrician, his parents seek help from a local counseling agency. The clinician engages the parents as facilitators, then Marcus's teacher, helping them to provide scaffolding that supports Marcus's goal orientation.

Child's role: Marcus understands that he has difficulty with task completion and learns to use a specific mediator (a "game plan") to provide scaffolding for his goal orientation.

Chapter 10: Connor, Age 9, Third Grade

Clinician's role: The clinician becomes involved when the parents seek help specifically for social skill problems and impulsive behavior. The clinician engages Connor as an active participant in his own treatment, with his parents in supporting roles as facilitators and coaches. Connor's treatment focuses primarily on response inhibition.

Child's role: Connor is very much involved as an active partner in setting up interventions to improve his response inhibition and other functions.

Chapter 11: Jon, Age 10, Fifth Grade

Clinician's role: The clinician becomes involved when Jon's mother, Mia, seeks help after learning about executive function from Jon's school counselor. Mia is already providing extensive scaffolding. The clinician helps them plan a way for Mia to scale back on the scaffolding and for Jon to take on more responsibility for strengthening, and providing external support for, his working memory.

Child's role: Jon is involved as an active partner. He also begins to develop a long-term vision for coping with his limitations.

CHAPTER EIGHT

Amanda, Age 4, Preschool

Executive Functions Involved: Shifting Focus

The capacity to shift focus means that we can change our perspectives and actions in response to changing events or new information. It entails:

1. Self-monitoring (the use of working memory to determine if one's ongoing response is suitable for the circumstances)
2. Interruption of the ongoing response if it is not
3. Cognitive and behavioral flexibility (considering and then choosing alternative ways of perceiving or behaving)

For children who have difficulty shifting focus, the behavioral expectations of the classroom can be frustrating. In school, children are expected to make multiple transitions: Upon a signal from the teacher, they are expected to interrupt an ongoing activity (which they may be enjoying very much) and switch to a new activity. They are also expected to be able to think flexibly—to see beyond their own self-interest, view a situation from the perspective of another child or of classroom rules, and behave in accordance with that larger perspective. In preschool classrooms, children are still learning to adapt to these behavioral expectations. They are not expected to independently monitor their own behavior. Preschool teachers expect to frequently remind the children of rules and expectations and to give emotional support and encouragement as children struggle with the inherent challenge of forgoing their own self-interests. With that support from the teacher, however, preschoolers are expected to be able to interrupt an inappropriate response upon request and to bring their actions in line with classroom expectations.

Summary of Previous Interventions

Four-year-old Amanda is having much greater difficulty than her classmates in meeting expectations at preschool. She is easily upset by the actions of other children and responds by either isolating herself or trying to direct the other child's behavior. If her attempts to direct another child meet with resistance, she reacts with verbal or physical aggression. When a teacher intervenes she often escalates the aggressive behavior, culminating in an emotional meltdown when the teacher removes her from the situation. Amanda also frequently resists following the teacher's instructions when that entails stopping an activity that she is absorbed in.

Amanda began preschool in August with Ms. Blum. As described in Chapters 3 and 6, from the first week of school, Ms. Blum identified two problem behaviors in Amanda: not keeping her hands to herself and not following the teacher's instructions. Ms. Blum tried a number of interventions, including reminders, redirection, time out, and, finally, a daily report sent to Amanda's parents. None of the interventions resulted in a change in the problem behaviors. The daily report was still in place when Ms. Blum took maternity leave in early October. When Ms. LeBlanc took over the classroom, she discontinued the daily report and began an informal assessment of Amanda's development (see Chapter 6).

Mental Health Clinician's Role

The mental health clinician is a monthly consultant to the preschool that Amanda attends. The clinician works with Amanda's teacher to design classroom-based interventions to support her response inhibition and shifting focus. They see significant improvement in the presenting problem, over a relatively short period of time, once the classroom-based interventions were changed.

In mid-October, after Ms. LeBlanc has begun her assessment, she speaks with the school's director. The director arranges to utilize the services of the school's mental health consultant, who visits the school monthly.

At the end of October, the consultant meets with the director and learns the history of Amanda's behavior and the interventions attempted by the previous teacher, along with the impressions Ms. LeBlanc has gathered from her recent informal assessment. He then observes Amanda for an hour in the classroom, including the Stop and Go game. He meets briefly with Ms. LeBlanc and suggests some changes to the game in order to provide a slightly different context for observing Amanda's response. This will enable them to determine whether Amanda will be able to respond to the stop cue even if the other children continue their activity. The consultant also encourages Ms. LeBlanc's plan of arranging for Amanda to engage in pretend play with small groups of children, including Celia (see Chapter 6). They make plans to meet the following month, review Amanda's response to the new context, and then formulate a more detailed intervention plan.

The following day, Ms. LeBlanc introduces the recommended change. When she leads Stop and Go at circle time, she now targets the cue to one child at a time, by saying that child's name before giving the cue. She continues to give both a verbal cue (the word *stop*) and a visual cue (the stop sign). Now, only the targeted child freezes while the other children continue moving to the music. During the delay provided by the freeze, Ms. LeBlanc goes to that child and talks quietly, complimenting his or her skills in stopping on cue, and asking a brief question before releasing the child (by saying "Go" and returning the stop sign to its hiding place behind her back). In this way, she sets up a system of having one child stop on cue and converse with her while the other children continue with their activity. She notes that Amanda is able to do this, and is able to converse quietly with her, even though the music and the other activity continue.

As noted in Chapter 6, part of what the facilitator does in a dynamic assessment is to create contexts for the purpose of learning more about the child's level of assisted development. In the Stop and Go game, Ms. LeBlanc learned that Amanda was capable of interrupting an ongoing response and then protecting the period of delay, in the context of a shared game. Amanda also followed the teacher's instructions in a one-on-one situation, when Amanda was not distracted or upset by the behaviors of other children.

In the new context, in which one child inhibits response while the other children continue the activity, a higher level of self-control is required. The targeted child must (1) protect the period of delay in the midst of distraction, and (2) shift attention from the game to a conversation with the teacher. Amanda's performance in this new context yielded information related to one of her particular difficulties: shifting her attention away from the other children and focusing on what the teacher was saying. This is significant because Ms. LeBlanc's assessment has already revealed that when not distracted, Amanda is eager and willing to follow instructions. If Ms. LeBlanc can provide scaffolding that helps Amanda filter out distractions, they will be able to take advantage of her ability to follow instructions.

At the end of November, the consultant meets again with Ms. LeBlanc and the school director. Ms. LeBlanc reports Amanda's ability to interrupt her response and shift her attention.

They review the two situations in which Amanda has difficulty: (1) when another student is doing something (often minor) that bothers her, and (2) when the daily agenda calls for her to stop an activity that she is enjoying and switch to a different activity. They decide to initially target the first situation (her verbal and physical aggression) because it causes the most disruption in the classroom and interferes with her forming friendships with the other children.

They discuss the goal previously set: Amanda will keep her hands to herself. The consultant recommends setting a goal that focuses on improving the mental processes that underlie the problem behavior. Together they set a goal: Amanda will improve her ability to shift focus when she is distressed by the actions of other children.

Because the new goal focuses on internal mental processes rather than the resulting external behavior, it helps to guide the intervention away from rewarding or punishing behaviors and toward finding ways to guide behaviors as they are occurring. Amanda already knows that it is against the rules for her to tell other children what to do and to physically interfere with them. Other children in the classroom either have already internalized this rule or, like Celia (see Chapter 3), are able to shift their focus and comply when they are reminded by the teacher. Amanda, however, has neither ability. She needs more external support. The new goal will help the adults plan interventions that can provide that external support.

> They discuss Amanda's ability to interrupt an ongoing response and shift her attention in Stop and Go. The consultant recommends that Ms. LeBlanc take the cues from the game and use them in classroom situations when they want Amanda to shift focus. Ms. LeBlanc can cue Amanda to stop and then use her freeze response to remind her of the rule and its importance. The gamelike quality of freezing in response to her teacher's cue will, they hypothesize, provide sufficient external support.

While Ms. LeBlanc's game was a very creative way of allowing Amanda to demonstrate executive function skills, it would be premature to assume that just because Amanda shows self-control in the context of the game, she should now be able to spontaneously transfer those skills to other situations. An essential part of the facilitator's job is to use information gleaned from the dynamic assessment to construct scaffolding at the point of performance.

A point-of-performance intervention provides external support when and where the problem behavior occurs. The consultant suggests using the cue-and-response scenario that Amanda has learned in the game to elicit the behaviors they want to see in the classroom.

> The consultant gives Ms. LeBlanc suggestions for gradually introducing the cue into a variety of everyday situations before using it in more emotionally charged situations. He recommends introducing the intervention in three stages: first during routine classroom activities where there is no problem, and second, when she can catch Amanda at the beginning of an incident. Only after Amanda has success in these two contexts should Ms. LeBlanc continue to the third stage: using the intervention when Amanda's behavior has already escalated.

Part of the facilitator's job is to be sensitive to the unique pace of a child's learning. Therefore, the facilitator sequences interventions in small steps that build on previous success. In this case, the consultant suggests that Ms. LeBlanc use the intervention only in the first two contexts. At their next meeting, they can review Amanda's responsiveness and then discuss how to use it for the third stage.

> On the following day, Ms. LeBlanc tells the children that they will no longer play Stop and Go at circle time. Instead, they will begin a new Stop and Go game that they will play all day long. She says that sometimes during the day she will surprise a child by saying his or her name plus the word "Stop" and show a pocket-size stop sign. "It will be a lot harder to freeze," she tells them, "because you won't know

when I am going to call your name and give you the stop signal. It will be a surprise. But you have to be ready to do the same thing you've been doing at circle time." She explains that, as in the game, the other children are all to continue with whatever activity they are already doing.

Ms. LeBlanc now does this frequently throughout the day, targeting each child at different times during the week, always when the child is behaving appropriately. The intervention lasts just a few seconds, long enough for Ms. LeBlanc to give the child a compliment and converse briefly. When Amanda is the chosen student, Ms. LeBlanc always makes it a point to get eye contact before talking with her.

Once Ms. LeBlanc is sure that Amanda is able to inhibit her behavior under the new conditions, she moves to the second step. Now she begins to use the cue when she notices that Amanda is beginning to interfere with another child, but before the situation has escalated.

Ms. LeBlanc sees Amanda standing up and reaching across the table toward Drew's paper that he is coloring. "No, Drew," Amanda tells him, "that's not how. You have to color inside the lines."

Ms. LeBlanc sits down at the table next to Amanda. "Amanda, stop," she says, putting the small stop sign on the table. Amanda freezes. Ms. LeBlanc now describes the situation (the stimulus) and also Amanda's response: "Amanda, you saw that Drew was coloring outside the lines. You didn't like that and you started telling him how to color his page. But then you stopped yourself. I'm so glad that you stopped, Amanda, because now we can talk about the rule."

Ms. LeBlanc waits and makes eye contact with Amanda. "Remember the rule: It's okay to tell yourself what to do, but only the . . ." She waits for Amanda to fill in the correct word. "Teacher," says Amanda. "Right," says Ms. LeBlanc, "only the teacher can tell another child what to do." She smiles at Amanda. "Are you ready to follow that rule?" Amanda nods. "Good, Amanda." Ms. LeBlanc removes the stop sign and says, "Now go." She remains long enough to be sure Amanda has shifted her focus back to her own coloring.

Ms. LeBlanc is now using the Stop and Go intervention at the point of performance. The game-based freeze response creates a space in which Ms. LeBlanc can engage Amanda in a brief conversation that helps her shift her thoughts to the classroom rules. This support helps her to consciously make a choice to follow the rules.

As suggested by the consultant, Ms. LeBlanc uses this technique only when she catches Amanda during the early stages of interfering with other children, before verbal or physical conflict. For those instances, she and Ms. Dartez continue as they have previously—physically intervening and moving her away if needed.

They also continue using time out if Amanda physically hurts another child or is aggressive or defiant with the teacher. However, the school director has introduced a change in the time out procedure for all of the children. A child-sized rocking chair is placed in the classroom and the children are told that it is "the relaxing chair." Ms. LeBlanc puts a bin by the chair with a teddy bear, a touch-and-feel book, a pillow, soft blanket, and other items that the children can use for self-soothing. She tells the children that they may use the chair to relax and calm down any time they feel "upset or grumpy." Now when she or Ms. Dartez has to intervene with Amanda, they take her hand and lead her to the relaxing chair, telling her, "When we get upset, we need to relax and calm down." The first few times, they sit with Amanda and actively coach her on self-calming skills: taking a deep breath, telling herself, "It's okay."

This is an excellent change in the time out procedure, which now encourages behaviors that promote cognitive and behavioral flexibility. Previously Amanda has self-soothed by sucking her finger and stroking her clothing (Chapter 3). These new behaviors—particularly the use of private speech and breathing—provide Amanda with more mature ways to soothe herself.

Ms. LeBlanc continues the intervention at the second level for 3 weeks, until she meets with the consultant in mid-December, shortly before the school is closed for the holidays. She reports success with the Stop and Go intervention when problem behaviors are beginning. Also, the relaxing chair is proving to be a big help when Amanda is upset. She and Ms. Dartez still need to intervene physically but spend less time calming Amanda down. She is now able to do some of that on her own. The consultant recommends that Ms. LeBlanc move to the third level of intervention—using Stop and Go when Amanda is upset—after classes resume in January.

At the end of January, Ms. LeBlanc reports that Amanda is doing surprisingly well. She is playing with other children at center time more often; previously she had preferred to be alone. Ms. LeBlanc explains that, after the first time Amanda engaged in pretend play with Celia, Emma, and Drew (Chapter 6), Amanda sought out opportunities for more pretend play, but only with Celia. Now, however, Amanda is beginning to play with other children as well, even children with whom she has conflicts during other class activities. Ms. LeBlanc notes that Amanda seems calmer and shows more flexibility in pretend play than during other classroom activities. It appears that when she is engrossed in a role, she is less disturbed by the actions of the other children, including behaviors that would upset her in ordinary activities.

As we noted in Chapter 5, the pretend play of preschoolers can give us a glimpse of the future child. While Amanda is still easily disturbed during regular classroom activities, she shows a higher level of cognitive and behavioral flexibility when she and the other children are engaged in imaginary play. According to Vygotsky's theory, this new level of functioning will soon be integrated into her everyday functioning.

During other classroom activities, Ms. LeBlanc has been able to scale back the scaffolding that she provides when Amanda begins to interfere with another child. She can say, "Amanda, stop," and then "Remember the rule" and "Go." Amanda can shift her focus without any additional external support.

Also, the frequency of Amanda's verbal or physical aggression has dropped from multiple times per day to about once per day. Because of this change, Ms. LeBlanc does not use the Stop and Go intervention for these situations. When Amanda begins to escalate her behavior, the teachers ask her if she needs to go to the relaxing chair. Amanda either willingly goes or shifts her focus without actually needing to use the chair; the reminder is sufficient.

Ms. LeBlanc tells the consultant that they are now con-

cerned about a new behavior. Amanda is coming to the
teachers frequently and tattling on the other children for
minor offenses. For example, in just the brief time since
school had begun that morning, Amanda complained to Ms.
Dartez that Lucy was singing too loudly and to Ms. LeBlanc
that Drew and Owen were hiding under the table.

The tattling may actually be a sign of progress in Amanda's
executive functioning. What Amanda is reporting, although
minor to the adults, is probably the type of behaviors that
have always bothered her. She now appears to be interrupting
her own prepotent response—she is no longer isolating herself
or being as bossy—and coming to her teachers for help in
managing her emotions. When Amanda began the school
year, this classroom rule about not interfering with other children was something imposed from without, not something
that guided her from within. With the external support provided by Ms. LeBlanc, she now appears to have internalized
this rule. Whereas many of her classmates may have internalized it quickly and easily, Amanda needed much more time
and external support.

> The consultant suggests that the teachers welcome Aman-
> da's tattling as an opportunity to help her think more flexi-
> bly about the other children and their actions. Rather than
> reprimanding her for tattling, they can try to help her figure
> out what to do. If Lucy is singing too loudly, how far away
> does Amanda need to move so it's not so loud? If Drew and
> Owen are hiding under the table, who are they hiding from?
> Is it a game? Would Amanda like to play with them?
> Through conversations with her teachers, Amanda may
> learn how to consider multiple points of view when events
> upset her.

Amanda is actively seeking out the type of shared activity that is hypothesized to provide the groundwork for internalized self-regulation (see Chapter 5). In this case, the shared activity is the use of language to help her shift focus and think flexibly. Just as she needed extra support to internalize the rule and stop her initial response to upsetting situations, she may also need extra support to think more flexibly about events. According to Bodrova and Leong, "children learn to use a mental process by sharing, or using it when interacting with others" and only after this period of shared experience "can the child internalize and use the mental process independently" (2007, p. 11).

By the end of the school year, the director reports to the consultant that Amanda's behavior is not any more problematic than that of other children in her class. She still has some difficulty with transitions from one activity to another, but she is never physically aggressive and her disagreements with the other students are normal ones for her age group.

Summary

- Problem: Four-year-old Amanda was easily distressed by the actions of her classmates and either isolated herself or attempted to direct them, often becoming verbally and physically aggressive. When her teachers intervened, she escalated the behaviors and often had an emotional meltdown when she was removed from the situation.
- Goal: Amanda will improve her ability to shift focus when she is distressed by the actions of other children.
- Facilitators: Amanda's classroom teacher, Ms. LeBlanc, was the primary facilitator. The school's mental health consultant and director were also involved in planning interventions.

- Dynamic assessment: The facilitators created contexts for assessing Amanda's level of assisted performance. The Stop and Go game, in different forms, provided contexts for assessing Amanda's ability to interrupt an ongoing response, protect the period of delay, and shift focus. The Stop and Go cues, without the game, provided an additional context for observation.

- Point-of-performance interventions: Ms. LeBlanc provided external support for Amanda's weak executive function (shifting focus). When Amanda was distressed, the Stop and Go cues provided scaffolding that helped her interrupt her response and consider and choose other responses. Later, the relaxing chair served as a mediator that supported her emotional self-regulation. When Amanda began tattling about other children, her teachers engaged her in a shared mental process (shared cognitive flexibility), helping her to think differently and more creatively.

- Other interventions and amplification: Amanda engaged in pretend play with peers, which appeared to support her emerging cognitive flexibility. Ms. LeBlanc's ongoing dynamic assessment also provided for exchange of information with Amanda's parents, which led to changes at home (see Chapter 6).

- Results: The dynamic assessment began in mid-October and the point-of-performance interventions began at the end of November. By the end of the school year, Amanda's ability to shift focus in response to peer-related difficulties was completely satisfactory. This case shows significant changes brought about by a teacher-initiated assessment and classroom-based interventions.

CHAPTER NINE

Marcus, Age 7, Second Grade

Executive Functions Involved: Goal Orientation

Goal orientation is the most complex of the executive function components. It is the ability to make a plan for achieving a goal, and then to hold that information in mind as one activates and executes all aspects of the plan. It builds on the foundational components (working memory, response inhibition, and shifting) and also includes a sense of time and an ability to motivate oneself to meet the goal in a timely fashion. Essentially, goal orientation means having an internal guide that allows for purposeful, flexible, goal-directed, and timely behavior.

We can readily appreciate the importance of goal orientation for academic tasks. Children who lack goal orientation are sometimes labeled by parents and teachers as lazy, uncaring, or unmotivated. All of these terms foster a view that the child is being willfully irresponsible. While poor goal orientation is particularly evident in the school setting, it can cause problems in a variety of daily activities—from cleaning one's room to getting ready for bed at night.

Summary of Previous Interventions

Seven-year-old Marcus (Chapter 3) is falling behind in Ms. Washington's second grade classroom because he is unable to complete independent seat work. Ms. Washington has warned Marcus's parents, Susan and Al, that he might not be able to move on to third grade unless he shows some improvement. Susan and Al set up a system of rewards and punishments to try to influence Marcus to show more responsibility. After following the program faithfully for 3 weeks, with no improvement, Susan and Al become increasingly frustrated with Ms. Washington, with Marcus, and with each other. Finally they decide to seek help from Marcus's pediatrician.

Mental Health Clinician's Role

The clinician becomes involved when, upon advice from the child's pediatrician, Susan and Al seek help from a local counseling agency. The clinician engages first the parents and later Marcus's teacher as facilitators, helping them to provide scaffolding that supports Marcus's goal orientation. This example shows significant improvement in a school-based presenting problem using a team approach and designing interventions that provide external support for Marcus's goal orientation.

> Two days after Susan and Al's decision to seek help, Susan brings their pediatrician up to date on Marcus's school difficulties and the family's failure to find a solution. She tearfully relates the arguments that she and her husband are having. She wants to increase rewards and punishment and is also willing to consider medication. Her friend's child, also a patient of this pediatrician, was placed on medication this

year and it has made a big difference. Al, however, is ada-mantly opposed to medication and wants to transfer Marcus to a different school. Susan does not want to move Marcus without moving his older sister, Olivia; but Olivia is having a great year and it seems unfair to make her move.

The pediatrician listens, sympathizes, and suggests that they not make any immediate decisions. She recommends that they first speak with a therapist at a local family coun-seling agency. He can help them understand why Marcus is having these problems and then help them sort through their options.

Susan calls the agency and makes an appointment for her and Al to meet with the therapist the following week. Fol-lowing this initial meeting, the therapist has a phone consul-tation with Ms. Washington and three 45-minute sessions with Marcus.

The therapist is beginning to conduct a dynamic assessment to understand not only Marcus's level of independent per-formance in completing assignments, but also his level of assisted performance. He gathers information about the problem behavior as presented by Ms. Washington but also about the contexts in which Marcus does complete school-work. He gathers information directly from Marcus during the three individual sessions, using a variety of games and activities designed to build rapport, to observe Marcus's be-havior, and to explore Marcus's perception of his school and family environments.

At the first session with Marcus, the therapist gives the fam-ily a home assignment: He asks them to begin conducting weekly family meetings. He explains he gives this assignment to all families, as a way of improving communication and problem-solving skills. He provides them with step-by-step instructions on holding a family meeting and asks that they take notes (see Figure 9.1) at their meetings and bring the notes to their therapy sessions.

The therapist immediately begins to engage the family in the habit of taking some sort of action between sessions. Some parents come into therapy thinking that the therapist will just talk with their child, and that being told what to do by an expert will be enough to motivate their child. However, because of the importance of developing new contexts for planning point-of-performance interventions, the therapist makes home assignments part of therapy from the start.

> After completing several individual sessions with Marcus, the therapist begins educating the parents about executive functions, with emphasis on goal orientation. He also begins to gently challenge their belief that Marcus just doesn't care. He points out that the two of them, along with Marcus's teacher and Marcus himself, have presented ample evidence that Marcus very much wants to please the adults in his life. For example, Marcus is always delighted when they are pleased with his work and feels sad when he does not meet their expectations. The therapist explains Marcus's performance in terms of his ZPD (see Figure 9.2). If an adult sits with him and guides him step by step, he finishes his work easily and is not resistant to the task. When working with a buddy the previous year, though sometimes inattentive, he always had a good attitude about the work and often helped his partner understand some of the more difficult concepts. By means of this conversation, the parents are able to see

Make a Plan During the week, use this space to write down questions, problems, and plans that might be discussed at the next family meeting.

AGENDA

☐ _____

☐ _____

☐ _____

☐ _____

☐ _____

☐ _____

On the day of the meeting, put a check by the topics that you want to discuss.

Meeting Format

1. Compliments.
Say thanks to each other for good deeds done or for help given during the week. You can also acknowledge accomplishments and encourage efforts.

2. Minutes.
Read minutes of the last meeting. Have plans that you made been working?

3. Old Business. Topics from last meeting can be discussed further.

4. New business. Discuss new topics, questions, complaints, or problems listed on the **AGENDA.**

5. Fun.
After the meeting is adjourned, stay together for a game, outing, or a dessert. Enjoy each other's company!

FIGURE 9.1. A family meeting agenda.

Date of Meeting: _____

MINUTES

Topics discussed:

Decisions made:

1 _____

_____

2 _____

_____

3 _____

_____

4 _____

_____

Adapted from **Treasure Time: A Game to Teach Social Skills and Family Meetings**

© 2006 Golden Path Games

FIGURE 9.1. continued.

Brainstorm!

If your family has a problem that is tough to resolve, brainstorm for solutions. Brainstorming is a creative process, in which no idea is considered wrong.

Here's how:

1) On the back of this page, write down any and all ideas that family members can come up with. **Don't reject *any* ideas** during this stage. Sometimes a silly idea leads to another idea, which leads to the perfect solution! (Try to come up with at least 5 ideas; 10 is even better.)

2) After the brainstorming is complete, go through the list and discuss the **pros and cons** of each idea. Give everyone a chance to speak.

3) Decide on a plan and try it out. If it doesn't work, bring the topic up again at another meeting. Keep working on it. Don't give up. **Every problem has a solution!**

165

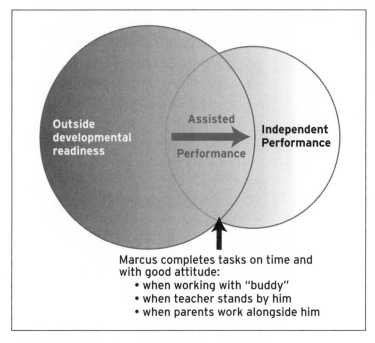

FIGURE 9.2. Marcus's ZPD for task completion.

clearly that their son enjoys learning and wants to do well–a far cry from someone who just doesn't care. What had appeared to them as a lack of caring is instead his developmental immaturity in the realm of goal orientation.

The concept of ZPD gives us a larger perspective on the child's development. Rather than thinking that the child won't perform or will never perform, the ZPD allows us to see that some abilities are emerging. The therapist makes the analogy of a child riding a bike (see Chapter 7). While Marcus bounds ahead of his peers in some areas–math and athletic skills, for example, are definitely in his level of independent performance—he lags behind in others. The difference isn't due to anything Marcus, the school, or the parents have done wrong. His brain is still maturing and it might be some time before his executive functioning catches up with that of his peers.

Marcus's parents readily understand this concept of differing rates of development. They comment that Marcus easily learned to ride a two-wheeler at age 4, while his older sister did not learn until age 7, and then with some difficulty. However, despite these very different learning curves, both children are avid and happy bike riders now. The parents conclude on their own that it makes no more sense to punish Marcus for his present difficulty than it would have made to punish their daughter for her failure to develop the sense of balance she needed to ride a bicycle.

The therapist agrees. In either case, what is needed is external support until the child has the right combination of neurological maturity and life experience that will allow him to finally achieve mastery. The task for the adults is to figure out ways to provide the right amount of external support for his emerging ability. The parents express some resentment that the teacher no longer allows Marcus to use the buddy system. However, the therapist expresses confidence that they can work together and find some other form of external support that will be as good as, or better than, the previous arrangement.

The therapist gives an example of a way to provide external support for goal orientation. During his three sessions with Marcus, he began each session by using a game plan (see Figure 9.3). The game plan broke their time together into segments, with a game or activity linked to each segment. This provided a visual map of what Marcus should ex-

FIGURE 9.3. Marcus's game plan.

pect in each session and helped him to make a smooth transition from one activity to the next. He actually used a game piece and moved it along so he could see where they were and what they had left to do. Furthermore, at the third session, Marcus entered the office and immediately said, "Let's make a game plan." He offered ideas and helped to write out the steps of the plan.

The therapist has created a context to observe Marcus's level of assisted performance. Marcus not only enjoys using the game plan but has begun to look forward to helping the therapist create it at the start of each session. Marcus is actively participating in formulating the plan and, when reminded, he checks the plan and tracks his progress.

Susan thinks that the game plan idea might help Marcus clean his room at home. If she doesn't stay in the room with him, it takes him 2 hours just to put his toys and games away, and his dirty clothes are still on the floor. The therapist points out the similarity between this behavior and Marcus's failure to complete work at school. This is a connection that the parents have not made. They have been viewing Marcus's difficulties as just a school problem.

Marcus's parents are beginning to apply what they have learned about executive function to everyday situations. Viewing goal orientation as a difficulty that affects Marcus in multiple domains increases their motivation to find solutions. His mother's use of the game plan concept at home creates a new context for assessing Marcus's level of assisted performance in planning and self-monitoring.

The parents also report that they have conducted two family meetings, and they bring their notebook with the completed agendas. The therapist points out that this is another way of helping Marcus acquire a concept of planning. He recommends that they allow Marcus and his sister to take turns writing up the agenda (the equivalent of creating steps for a plan) and recording the decisions that they made (the equivalent of following steps in a plan) and also reading the notes from the last session (a type of self-monitoring).

The family meeting provides another context to assess Marcus's ability to plan and monitor actions.

At the next therapy session, Marcus and his mother report on their experience in using the game plan to help Marcus stay on track while cleaning his room. They used a game board that they already had at home, one with start and finish spaces. Then, using sticky notes, they wrote down each task that Marcus needed to complete. Susan then helped him put the sticky notes on the game board between the start and finish spaces, in the order that she wanted the tasks done. She added another sticky note as the last item: She and Marcus would play his favorite game in his newly cleaned room. She checked on Marcus every 5 minutes and made sure that he was moving his game marker from one space to the next as he progressed.

They report to the therapist that Marcus finished the tasks in just under 30 minutes and that they then spent another 30 minutes playing his favorite game. It was an all-time record for speed and a first-ever happy ending for that particular chore.

Susan speaks privately with the therapist and tells him that she and her husband talked again with Marcus's teacher. They shared what they were learning and what they were doing at home, and Ms. Washington expressed interest in getting suggestions from the therapist.

It is not until this point that the therapist begins to plan an intervention to directly address the problem of poor school performance. This is an example of sequencing interventions. The same intervention (the game plan) is used in multiple contexts, beginning with the easiest one and moving to more difficult contexts (see Table 9.1). By using the intervention first in the less difficult contexts, Marcus experiences success, and his confidence in using the intervention will help him in the next, more challenging context.

At the next session, when Marcus and his therapist make their game plan for that day, the therapist writes in the first blank space: "Talk about school." When Marcus moves his marker from the start space to this first space, the therapist says, "Let's talk about school. Your teacher and your parents are worried. They've noticed that you are having a hard time getting your work done at school. They want to find a way to help you."

The therapist shows Marcus a worksheet that Marcus's parents brought to him. When they talk about it, Marcus can easily see his errors, but he cannot reflect on how he made the errors. It is a mystery to him why he was unable to complete the task in class.

The therapist asks, "Marcus, the next time that you have to do work like this at school, what would you like to have happen?" After a bit of discussion, Marcus is able to verbalize a goal: to get the work done, not to be the last one done, not to have to stay in for recess.

TABLE 9.1. Sequencing Interventions: Use of the Game Plan to Scaffold Performance in Different Contexts

Sequence/ Context	How Intervention Was Used	Level of Difficulty
First level of intervention: Therapist's office	**Therapist** and **Marcus** use a game plan to plan and track the activities used during the therapy sessions.	**Easy:** • Few distractions • One-on-one interaction • Mostly fun activities
Second level of intervention: Home	**Marcus** and **his mother** use a game plan to create a visual plan for Marcus to follow in cleaning his room.	**Medium:** • More distraction • Mother helps him create the plan, but leaves him mostly on his own to follow through • Activities (chores) are not things he is highly motivated to do (but a reward activity is built into plan)

The therapist then provides a blank copy of same worksheet and tells Marcus that today they will use a special game plan to help him finish it. He explains that the worksheet has a start and a finish and steps in between, just like the game plan that they have been using. "Can you see them?" the therapist asks. Marcus cannot. "I'm going to show you where they are," says the therapist.

He has prepared cutouts of the game plan segments: one start space, five blank spaces, and one finish space (see Figure 9.4). He hands the start space to Marcus and asks him to put it by the written instructions at the top of the page. "This is where you have to start, because even though you hear the teacher say the instructions, it's important to read the instructions also. If what you read doesn't match what you heard, ask your teacher for help. Before you move off start, whisper to yourself what you have to do to finish the worksheet."

Next the therapist asks Marcus to count the sentences on the worksheet. Marcus replies that there are five. The therapist hands him the five blank spaces and instructs him to put one by each of the five sentences. "These are the things that you need to do with this game plan. You will have 10 minutes to get all of these done."

Next, he gives Marcus the cutout finish space and has him place it at the bottom of the page. "When you get down to the finish space, you'll know that you got the job done," says the therapist. "Remember that at the start space, you whispered to yourself what to do. What would be a good thing to whisper to yourself after you get the job done?" After more discussion, Marcus decides he could whisper to himself, "Good job, I got the work done." The therapist has Marcus write these words on the worksheet, next to the finish space.

The therapist has Marcus choose a game piece and then instructs him to follow the game plan. Marcus is able to quickly, and correctly, complete the worksheet this time, although the therapist has to remind him to move his marker. When he moves the marker to the finish space, the therapist asks him to read the words aloud. "Good job, I got the work done!" Marcus smiles.

FIGURE 9.4. Game plan segment cutouts.

Because Marcus does not have a strong internal guide for task completion, the therapist has externalized his goal orientation function for the purpose of completing the worksheet. Many experts emphasize that we should expect that children with weak executive functioning will need to rely on external sources of support in more situations, and for a longer developmental period, than children with strong functioning (Barkley, 1997; Berk, 1994).

On Friday morning, the therapist and Ms. Washington have a phone consultation about Marcus's difficulty with staying on track toward a goal. Ms. Washington knows that Marcus's parents are not pleased that she has withdrawn the buddy system, but she thinks it is important that Marcus learn to work independently. If not, he'll be totally lost in third grade, she says.

The therapist asks whether the children ever play board games in her classroom. They do, and Ms. Washington relates that Marcus is strong in math and loves to play math board games. In such games, Marcus is very competitive, very focused, knows the materials, and outshines the other students. "There's no problem then with his staying focused," she says, "so that's how I know he could do the seat work if he wants to. He just has to make up his mind to do it."

The therapist expresses uncertainty that Marcus can simply "make up his mind" to work independently. He explains his hypothesis that Marcus's executive functions—particularly those related to goal orientation—are not as developed as those of his peers. It seems likely that the board game format and social interaction provide the right amount of external support to keep Marcus on track. If the therapist's hypothesis is correct, it would be impossible for Marcus to achieve the same level of independent work as his peers without some form of external support.

Ms. Washington sees his point, but states that she cannot always arrange for him to work with other students. The therapist wonders if they might be able to find some other way to give Marcus external support. The therapist tells Ms. Washington about how he applied the game plan concept to one of worksheets that Marcus had struggled with in her class. He emphasized that clearly delineating the directions with a start sign and allowing Marcus to use a marker to track his progress appeared to help him focus. Would she be willing to give that intervention a try in the classroom?

Ms. Washington agrees that the game plan concept may help Marcus to better visualize what he needs to do during independent assignments. She thinks it is worth a try. The therapist e-mails her a copy of the worksheet/game plan that he and Marcus created in his office.

The therapist is offering a concrete strategy that has already proved successful in two contexts: enlisting Marcus's cooperation in therapy sessions and helping Marcus complete a multistep task at home (cleaning his room).

On Monday morning, Ms. Washington meets privately with Marcus. She shows him the worksheet that the class will be using that afternoon. "I am going to help you make a game plan for your worksheet," she tells him. "This game plan will help you stay on track and finish your work on time."

The teacher uses language similar to what the therapist had used, and draws a start space by the directions, one space next to each item, and a finish space at the bottom of the page. "When you get to that space, you'll know you are

finished," she tells him. "You've won the game! Yahoo!" She
writes "YAHOO!" in big letters and they both laugh. "Let's
see, you'll need a game piece for your game plan, right?" She
allows him to choose one of the colorful erasers she keeps in
her desk drawer to mark his progress.

After Ms. Washington has drawn game plans on Marcus's
worksheets for 3 weeks, he has made one big improvement.
He is reliably reading the written directions and his work
now is almost always completed correctly. Ms. Washington
has even begun to give Marcus the responsibility for creating
the plan. She has him draw the game plan on his own worksheet. She checks to make sure it is done correctly before he
begins. In this way she is gradually removing the scaffolding.

However, Marcus still struggles with completing the work
in a timely manner. He often seems to be daydreaming and
looking around the classroom. Ms. Washington decides to
speak with the school's educational strategist.

The strategist hypothesizes that Marcus's current problem
might be a poor sense of time, combined with a less than
stellar ability to self-monitor. Although Marcus is using the
colorful eraser to track his progress, he still looks around the
room at other students, perhaps an indication that he is using their actions to prompt him to complete his work.

The strategist suggests that Ms. Washington place a small
timer on Marcus's desk to help him be more cognizant of
the passage of time. She recommends that Marcus be instructed not to look around the room. Instead, he should
concentrate on the timer, his game plan, and his game piece.
The strategist also suggests that the teacher give Marcus
permission to "talk to himself" about what he needs to do

each step of the way. Ms. Washington can practice with him and show him how to talk to himself in a quiet, almost silent voice that will not disturb other students.

The strategist has helped Ms. Washington externalize two other components of goal orientation: internalized language and time management. Ms. Washington begins to implement this plan and also contacts Marcus's therapist to give a progress report and to pass along the recommendations of the strategist.

> At his next meeting with Marcus's parents, the therapist discusses the new interventions that Ms. Washington has implemented. He suggests that the parents might want to find ways to reinforce these abilities at home: maintaining an awareness of the passage of time and monitoring progress within that time frame. The therapist points out that often the best way for children to learn skills is by doing something that seems fun to them but requires the skills, so that they are practicing the skills without even realizing it.
>
> One thing that Marcus enjoys doing on weekends is riding in the car with his father to run errands—to the garden center, to the car wash, to visit his grandparents, and so on. The parents decide that, prior to leaving, Marcus will help his father make a game plan for that day's activities. Also, his father will try to guess how long each activity will take, and Marcus will write that estimate on the game plan. Then Marcus will time each errand with a stopwatch and write the actual time on the game plan. They will make a game of it and call it Beat the Clock.

Setting up a context at home that echoes the challenges at school is an example of amplification within the child's ZPD (see Chapter 5). This new context is playful and fun and engages Marcus's interest. By adding new contexts that allow the child to practice the targeted skill in developmentally appropriate ways, Marcus's parents are laying a firm foundation for future development.

By the end of April, Marcus is consistently bringing home correct and complete schoolwork. Ms. Washington has told Marcus's parents that she still has to call his attention to the timer and remind him to talk to himself. But she and Marcus have worked out a cue to use as a reminder that redirects him with relatively little disruption to the rest of the classroom. She thinks that even if he still needs these supports next year, it will be reasonable to expect the third grade teacher to provide them.

Ms. Washington is satisfied with Marcus's performance, and his parents are pleased that their frustration is gone. Furthermore, they are pleased that they have better insight into his development and they think that, with their understanding of Marcus's need for external support, they are much better equipped to handle any problems that might arise in the future.

Summary

- Problem: Seven-year-old Marcus was falling behind academically at school not because he did not know the subject matter but because of immature goal orientation. He could not plan a course of action and track his progress in carrying it out. Consequently, at school he was often doing tasks incorrectly and failing to complete them on time.
- Goal: Marcus will understand the concept of having a plan. He will acquire strategies to help him (1) create a plan and

(2) independently monitor his progress in completing the plan. He will utilize these strategies in his schoolwork.

- Facilitators: Marcus's therapist initially served as facilitator to cocreate a plan for the therapy session and to have Marcus monitor its implementation. Next, Marcus's mother served as facilitator at home, helping Marcus use those same strategies to create and implement a plan for cleaning his room. His teacher helped him utilize similar strategies in the classroom. His father gave him additional opportunities to use the strategies that he had learned.

- Dynamic assessment: The facilitators observed and created contexts for assessing Marcus's level of assisted performance. The therapist gathered information indicating that Marcus was very capable of completing multistep tasks when working with another person. The use of the game plan provided a context for assessing Marcus's ability to use an external mediator to self-monitor progress in following a step-by-step plan.

- Point-of-Performance Interventions: Ms. Washington provided scaffolding in the form of a game plan, coached Marcus to use private speech, and gave him a timer to externalize his sense of time.

- Other intervention and amplification: (1) Family meetings and (2) Beat the Clock game while running errands with his father.

- Results: At the beginning of the school year, goal orientation in the form of completion of seat work was within Marcus's ZPD—he could complete the work accurately and in a timely manner—but only when an adult or another student kept him on track. By May, Marcus was successfully using a mediator (the game plan) to help him with his goal orientation. His teacher and parents were satisfied with his progress.

CHAPTER TEN

Connor, Age 9, Third Grade

Executive Functions Involved: Response Inhibition

Response inhibition refers to a person's ability to stop himself from doing things that do not contribute to his intentions or goals. Suppressing one's natural, immediate response to a stimulus provides the opportunity to choose other, alternative responses. In the pause created by response inhibition, the person can use working memory to recall intentions and internalized language to reflect on the situation from different perspectives.

Response inhibition is important in almost all sectors of a child's life, none more so than social relationships. As children mature, they are increasingly expected to inhibit behaviors to create long-term benefits for themselves and others. Young children are expected to refrain from physical aggression such as hitting, pushing, and biting. As they grow older, they are also expected to refrain from impulsive actions that other people find annoying, rude, or socially inappropriate. The ability to pause allows children to understand the perspective of others and use negotiation to solve interpersonal problems.

Summary of Previous Interventions

Nine-year-old Connor is having difficulty in a variety of social situations because of impulsive behavior, including some problems with anger management and aggression. He acts like a much younger child, and although his friends tolerate some of his behaviors they are also beginning to avoid him, and he is not being invited to participate in activities as often as in the past. After his father, Jason, goes on a camping trip with Connor and other boys and fathers, he recognizes that his wife's concerns about Connor are valid. He decides to talk with her about getting some help for Connor.

Mental Health Clinician's Role

The clinician becomes involved when the parents seek help specifically for social skill problems and impulsive behavior. The clinician engages Connor as an active participant in his own treatment, with his parents in supporting roles as facilitators and coaches. After multiple interventions over an extended period of time, Connor shows significant improvement in his ability to take responsibility for his behavior and work with others to implement solutions.

Ginger, Jason's wife, tells him about a social skills therapy group that she has learned about through a friend. She contacts the therapist by phone and after a review of Connor's difficulties, the therapist sets up an initial meeting for the parents.

At that meeting, the therapist learns that Connor has always been very impulsive. Every year since kindergarten, Connor's teachers have told his parents that he has trouble keeping his hands to himself, staying in his seat, and waiting for his turn to speak. As Connor progressed in school, much of that behavior improved. He stays seated, does not blurt out answers, and completes his work, although it is often rushed and sloppy. Although he currently performs well in the classroom, he still has problems in less structured situations. On the playground and on field trips, he often pokes, pushes, and generally annoys other children.

Connor also has a history of being short tempered, and his parents are concerned that this problem is becoming worse. His friends seem less tolerant of his outbursts and also of him blurting out inappropriate things and acting silly. Both parents admit that they can understand the children's reluctance to include Connor. They themselves find him exhausting to be around. Jason tells the therapist that he was a lot like Connor as a child. He recalls being severely punished at both home and school for his inability to think before acting. He has tried to bring Connor up differently without being so punitive, but now he worries that he has been too lax and Connor doesn't know how to behave properly in social situations.

With this background information, the therapist hypothesizes that Connor's social skill problems are secondary to his poor impulse control. He educates Jason and Ginger about executive function and recommends that, prior to putting Connor in a social skills group, they begin with individual and family therapy to create some effective external support for Connor's poor response inhibition. Jason and Ginger agree and the therapist schedules a session for Connor and his parents.

At Connor's first session, after getting acquainted a bit in the waiting room, the therapist brings Connor and his parents to his office. Pointing to a "feelings poster" on the wall, he asks Connor to show him how he feels about being there. Connor points to the feeling "nervous." The therapist tells him that most people do feel nervous the first time they come to his office, and asks him to rate how nervous he feels, on a scale of 1 to 10. Connor replies, "I guess about a 7." After getting the parents to do the same thing, the therapist writes the words "A Safe Place" on a dry erase board and tells Connor that he hopes the office will be a safe place for him and his parents, where they can come and talk about any problems they might have and figure out ways that they can make their problems better. He says that he hopes by the time Connor leaves, he won't feel so nervous, maybe just a 6 instead of a 7, or maybe even a 5.

The therapist is beginning with an activity designed to assess Connor's ability to accurately identify his emotions. Based on information from Connor's parents and on Connor's body language, his selection of the word "nervous" and his intensity rating of a 7 on a 10-point scale seem accurate, and the therapist concludes that Connor seems to have a good awareness of his emotional state.

The therapist asks Connor to stand up and do "air angels" (see Activity 10.1). After he does three air angels, the therapist asks Connor to again rate how nervous he feels and Connor indicates a 5. The therapist explains that we experience our feelings not just in our heads but in our bodies as well, and just stretching and taking a deep breath can help us feel calmer.

The therapist immediately begins an active approach, teaching Connor an intervention that has a direct impact on his

Activity 10.1. Air Angels

RATIONALE: To be successful with self-calming, children need to be aware of how their bodies feel when they are tense or upset. This activity helps them learn to slow and deepen their breathing and relax their muscles.

GOAL: This activity helps to raise the child's awareness that self-calming is a skill that can be practiced and improved.

MATERIALS NEEDED: None.

EXPLANATION FOR CHILD: To do an air angel, you have to pay attention to two things: (1) your breath and (2) your body. You have to slow down your breath and relax your body.

"First, let's practice breathing. We will each take a deep breath and then let it out slowly. When we breathe out, let's see how long we can keep breathing out."

(Together with the child, take three deep breaths.)

"Next, let's relax our bodies by stretching and releasing our muscles. We are going to make air angels. Put your arms straight above your head and stretch your whole body up as tall as you possibly can. Hold that tight and then stretch a little more. Now, slowly lower your arms to your sides, like an angel's wings. As you slowly bring down your arms, breathe slowly out, and let your whole body relax."

Practice this several times. Make sure that the child really feels the difference between the **tension** with arms and body outstretched and the **release** of muscles as he relaxes his arms and body.

SUGGESTIONS FOR EXPANDING THE ACTIVITY: To help the child be more aware of his breath, have the child use a pinwheel during the out breath. Encourage him to see how long he can keep the pinwheel going.

With older children, you can use the terms *tension* and *release* and ask the child to rate the degree of tension and degree of release on a scale of 5 (very tense) to 1 (very relaxed).

Adapted from **Simon Says Pay Attention** (Cool-Down assignment), **p. 103, © Golden Path Games, 2009.**

physiological experience of anxiety. He also is introducing the idea of self-monitoring, which will be followed up in future sessions.

> The therapist next asks the family to explain why they are there. At the previous session, the therapist had made a plan with the parents regarding how to explain to Connor why they were coming to counseling. Now Jason speaks up and tells the therapist that he has already explained to Connor that Connor is a lot like he was as a boy, and sometimes does things without thinking. Jason says that it got him in a lot of trouble or made people mad at him. The therapist asks Jason how he felt when that happened. Jason replies, "I felt sad." Connor moves by his dad and snuggles up close to him. Jason puts his arm around Connor and says that he wants to help his son learn some ways to stop and think before he acts so he can make better choices.

Because they agreed beforehand how to discuss the reason for the current counseling, the topic is brought up in a way that is supportive of Connor. Jason first admits that he knows of this problem from firsthand experience, sending two messages: that this is a common problem and that he can personally empathize with Connor's experience. Had the therapist not prepared the parents beforehand, the topic may have been presented in a punitive or critical way. Instead, the initial discussion of the problem helps to foster a bond of understanding between father and son.

> The therapist asks for examples and Jason tells about the incident on the camping trip when Connor told his friends that he and his father had seen a bald eagle (see Chapter 3).

They discuss this, and Connor admits that he has no idea why he said it, and that once he said it, he thought he couldn't say that he had made it up, so he kept going and "made up more lies."

The therapist wants to use this incident to help Connor begin to set some therapeutic goals for himself, so he asks a series of questions:

Therapist: Connor, how did you feel when your dad talked with you afterward, and you told him you had no idea why you said that?

Connor: Bad.

Therapist: What kind of bad feeling? Do you see a word on the feelings poster that describes what kind of bad feeling it was?

Connor: Mmmmm. "Embarrassed" . . . and . . . "guilty."

Therapist: Now, let's imagine that you could go back in time, back to before you said that. What do you wish you had done instead?

Connor: I wish I had never said that.

Therapist: So, you wish that when your friends were talking about seeing birds, you could have stopped and thought before you said anything, and then you could have said something true instead of something not true?

Connor: Yeah.

Therapist: If you had stopped and thought about it before you spoke, what might you have thought of saying instead?

Connor: Um. I don't know.

Therapist: Let's pretend right now. I'll be your friend and I'll say the part about seeing hawks. This time after you hear that, you stop and think, and after you think, say something that is true.

Connor: Okay.

Therapist: Hey, Connor, my dad and I were camping and we had some binoculars and we saw some hawks.

Connor is silent and doesn't respond, so the therapist helps him out:

Therapist: Connor, what were you thinking when your friend said that?
Connor: I don't even have any binoculars. I never saw anything.
Therapist: Try saying that to me, then.
Connor: Um . . . I don't have any binoculars. I never saw any hawks.
Therapist: Well, I have some binoculars back at the campsite. Do you want to try them?
Connor: Yeah. Cool.

The therapist is setting the stage not only for response inhibition but for awareness of internalized language. The therapist continues the dialogue, because he wants to make Connor aware that if he is not able to inhibit the prepotent response, it is still possible to interrupt the ongoing response.

Therapist: How do you think that turned out, Connor, when you stopped and thought and said something true?
Connor: Pretty good!
Therapist: I think so, too. You did great. Now let's do that again, but this time let's do it a little differently. This time you be the friend and I'll be you. I'm going to say the same thing you said about the eagle, but then I am going to stop myself and say something true instead. Okay?
Connor: Okay.
Therapist: Okay, so go—I'm you and you tell me about seeing the hawks. Then I'll say I saw a bald eagle and you ask me a question, just like your friend did, okay?

Connor: Hey, Connor, I go camping all the time and I have binoculars and we saw some hawks.

Therapist: Well, my dad and I saw some bald eagles.

Connor: Where did you see them?

The therapist now steps out of role momentarily and says as an aside to Connor and his parents: "Okay, now here's the tricky part. I said something that wasn't true. What should I do next? Keep on with the story? Or admit that I wasn't telling the truth? This is tough." The therapist pauses and Connor immediately speaks up: "You can say that you were just kidding!"

The therapist accepts Connor's suggestion and continues the dialogue:

Therapist: Uh, well, actually, I haven't seen any yet. I was just kidding. But I'd like to see a bald eagle. Have you ever seen one?

Connor: Um, no, I haven't seen any. But I have some binoculars. Maybe we can look for one.

Therapist: That would be cool.

The therapist knows that much of their initial work will center on helping Connor interrupt an ongoing response. It may be a long while before Connor is able to appropriately inhibit responses before they occur. This is part of the sequencing that will need to take place. The initial goal will be to engage Connor's parents as facilitators, to set up cues by which they can remind Connor of the need to inhibit a response, and for Connor to interrupt his response. To demonstrate the concept of interrupting an ongoing response, the therapist has Connor and his parents role-play this scene several more times, taking turns playing different roles. To add some fun, he uses a "director's clapboard" and says "cut" at the end of a role-play, and "Take two" and "Take three" at the beginning of a new role-play. Connor asks to be the director, and the therapist turns the clapboard over to him. In between takes, they talk about what happened in that scene, and the therapist introduces language that they will use in upcoming therapy sessions, such as, "He stopped and thought before he said anything" and "He knew that he was doing something wrong, so he stopped himself right away and did something different."

> The therapist begins to wrap up the session, thanking Connor for telling him about, and showing him, the problem he is having. He thanked him especially for sharing how he felt about the problem: embarrassed and guilty. Pointing to the words written on the board, he says he is glad that Connor felt safe enough to explain his problem and his feelings. "The good news," he tells Connor, "is that your parents brought you to the right place. This is what I do all day long. I teach children skills to help them to stop themselves when they need to and think about what they really want to do. And we'll do lots of fun activities to practice those skills."
>
> The therapist introduces one last activity, a ball game in which Connor has to say "good things" about himself, his family, his school, and his friends, and say three things he wishes for himself and his family. As they prepare to leave, the therapist asks him to rate again how nervous he feels. Connor replies, "Two," and spontaneously points to another feeling on the poster: happy. "I feel this now. This was fun!"

In this first session, the therapist has (1) set the stage for Connor to own the problem, by directly acknowledging the problems that have brought him in for counseling; (2) begun the process of setting specific goals related to response inhibition (both inhibiting the prepotent response and interrupting an ongoing response); (3) established a plan of building on Connor's existing strengths; and (4) begun the process of involving parents as facilitators. All of this has been done using a developmentally appropriate approach: active, playful interventions that immediately engage Connor's interest and set the stage for him to become an active partner in the therapeutic process.

At their next session, with the parents present, the therapist begins with a game, Simon Says Don't Do It (see Activity 10.2). The primary purpose of this game is to introduce Connor to the concept of response inhibition. A secondary purpose is to teach the use of private speech to facilitate response inhibition.

> Connor and the therapist play the game. He is sent back to the start line two times, but then proceeds to the finish line. The therapist comments on his actions as he proceeds, saying things such as, "Good job, you stopped yourself from doing the wrong thing. . . . Excellent, you didn't move a muscle that time. . . . I can see you are thinking before you act."

When the game is played the second time, the therapist gives Connor a small card that says, "Don't Do It" (Figure 10.1).

> The therapist tells Connor that this time, he not only has to stop moving, but at the same time he must say to himself—out loud—the words "Don't do it!" If he doesn't remember to say "Don't do it!" then he will have to go back to the start line. He tells Connor that to make the game more difficult,

Activity 10.2. Simon Says Don't Do It!

GOAL: This activity introduces the concept of response inhibition and the use of private speech to support it.

RATIONALE: Research shows that effective internalized language helps with response inhibition.

BENEFIT: This activity raises the child's awareness that response inhibition is something that can be improved with the right strategies.

MATERIALS NEEDED: None for Part 1; Don't Do It card for Part 2.

EXPLANATION FOR CHILD: "The name of this activity is Simon Says Don't Do It! In this game, what you *don't* do is very important. You have to be very careful that you don't do the wrong thing— because guess what happens if you do? You have to go back and start all over again!"

INSTRUCTIONS: PART 1

1. Simon (initially, the therapist) stands on one side of the room (finish line) and the child stands on the other end of the room (starting line).

2. Simon gives a series of commands such as "Take three baby steps forward," "Jump up and down," "Twirl around," "Take one giant step forward," "Pat your head and rub your tummy," "Take two bunny hops forward," and so on. Sometimes Simon gives the command with the magic words, "Simon says." Sometimes Simon gives the command without saying the magic words. The child is to respond only when it is preceded by the magic words.

3. If the child responds without the magic words, he must return to the starting line.

Note: Go slowly and give the child a chance to succeed. However, try to trick the child into making at least one wrong move, so that he has the experience of going back to the starting line. Try to do this early on and then follow up more slowly, giving the child a chance to succeed. If the child starts to do the wrong thing and then stops himself, comment on it: "Good job! You remembered and you stopped yourself from responding. You are really paying close attention!"

4. Review: Tell the child, "You did a great job. You understand that sometimes what you don't do is very, very important. Sometimes you almost did the wrong thing, but then you remembered and you stopped yourself." Give a specific example. "That was excellent. Are you ready to make the game a little harder?"

EXPLANATION FOR CHILD: "We are going to play Simon Says again and we are going to do a few things differently. In this game, I am going to try really, really, really hard to trick you. Whenever I tell you to do something without saying "Simon says," I want you to whisper to yourself, "Don't do it!" In this game, if you move at the wrong time or if you forget to whisper "Don't do it!" you will have to go back to the starting line.

Give the child the Don't Do It card to hold during the game as a reminder. Have the child practice saying "Don't do it" in a whisper that is loud enough for you to hear.

INSTRUCTIONS: PART 2
In this version, Simon tries harder to trick the child. Some ways to do this are:
1. Sometimes begin the command with similar but different words (e.g., Slimon says, Pimon says, Simon suggests, Simon wants you to . . .).
2. Sometimes begin with the child' name (Marie, take one giant step forward).
3. Say, "Let's do this," and demonstrate a funny or silly move.

Note: The purpose of this game is for the child to use self-talk as an aid to inhibiting behavior. Respond to his actions in ways that raise his awareness of his ability to do this.
1. If the child remembers to whisper "Don't do it," be sure to acknowledge it: "Good job, you told yourself just what to do."
2. If the child starts to do the wrong thing and then stops himself and whispers "Don't do it," comment on it: "Good job! You told yourself to stop just in time."

(continued)

Activity 10.2. Continued

3. If the child fails to inhibit his behavior, or fails to whisper "Don't do it," comment on it: "Uh-oh, what did you forget to do? It's back to the starting line!" "Let's practice together. What do we need to tell ourselves when there is something we are not supposed to do?" Practice together. Feel free to ham it up and be silly: Make the game fun, even if the child has to start over again.

VARIATIONS: Have the parent join the child in the game. Give the child a turn to be Simon.

Adapted from **Simon Says Pay Attention** (Simon Says Don't Do It activity), **p. 58, © Golden Path Games, 2009.**

he is going to add some distractions—Connor's parents are going to play alongside him.

The therapist pays close attention as the game proceeds. Connor is having more difficulty now because sometimes his parents move at the wrong time and he has a tendency

FIGURE 10.1. Don't Do It card.

to automatically follow their lead. When the therapist sees this happening, he quickly intervenes, telling Connor, "Remember what to say!" This cues Connor to interrupt his response and say, "Don't do it!" There is lots of laughter when one of his parents has to go back to the start line while Connor maintains his place. When Connor remembers on his own to say "Don't do it!" the therapist compliments him: "Great job, Connor, you told yourself what to do."

In the context of the game, the therapist is demonstrating two things: Connor can use private speech to facilitate response inhibition and another person can provide scaffolding by reminding Connor to use private speech. The game is played again, with first Connor, then his parents, taking the therapist's position as the leader of the game. This gives Jason and Ginger practice in providing the scaffolding and the therapist an opportunity to see how Connor responds to it.

Once the game has been played several times, and everyone is seated again, the therapist places a stack of Don't Do It cards on the coffee table and says, "Let's talk about times in real life when we have to tell ourselves 'Don't do it.'" He takes the top card from the stack and says, "When I am driving home from work and someone pulls out in front of me, I think about saying some curse words, but then I tell myself 'Don't do it!' and I take a deep breath and listen to my music instead." Ginger goes next, picking up a card and saying, "When I get hungry in the afternoon and I think eating of some cookies, I tell myself 'Don't Do It!' and I eat some the pretzels or an apple instead." Jason talks about stopping himself from wasting time on the computer and Connor says he needs to say "Don't do it" when his little sisters are annoying and he needs to stop himself from yelling at them.

The therapist is clearly linking the skills practiced in the game with the need to use these skills in real-life situations. This is a step toward scaffolding at the point of performance.

> The therapist explains the concept of point of performance and then asks each person to think of a place to post the Don't Do It card so that it "can be a reminder to stop yourself from doing something." He again goes first and says that he could tape his card to his steering wheel to stop himself from getting angry in traffic. Ginger says that she could tape hers on her kitchen cabinets to stop herself from eating cookies. Jason says that he could tape his on his computer to stop himself from wasting time. Connor needs help in figuring out what to do with his, but after some discussion, decides that he could tape it on the television, to stop himself from yelling at his little sisters when they are being noisy when he is watching TV.
>
> The therapist asks all three of them to try it out at home, and then report back to him at his next session.

The therapist is beginning a process of giving home assignments to be carried out between sessions. Home assignments are essential; the therapist does not assume that just talking about a skill in the office, or practicing in a role-playing format, will result in changes in real-life situations. The home assignments provide the opportunity to practice the skill in real life. The therapist can next begin determining how much external support Connor will need to be able to practice response inhibition in those actual situations.

> At the next session, with Connor and his mother present, Connor tells the therapist that the Don't Do It card has

helped. He has been able to stop himself from yelling at his sisters, and he has been telling his mother instead. She affirms that he has been doing much better. In fact, they have all had fun with their assignments, making it a point of saying "Don't do it" out loud, so that the others can hear them doing it.

The therapist compliments Connor on his skills and says that they are now going to do some brainstorming. He puts seven Don't Do It cards on the table and asks Connor and Ginger to think of seven situations where Connor needs his Don't Do It skills. This time he wants them to write the situations on the cards. The seven situations they come up with are arguing about bedtime, teasing his sisters after being asked to stop, getting mad and stomping off when things don't go his way, lying about brushing his teeth, kicking the back of his mom's seat in the car, begging his parents to buy him something in the store, and talking too loudly in church.

They consider these problems one by one and discuss whether taping up a Don't Do It card would work in these other situations. That is, is there a way to post a visual reminder at the point of performance to help Connor remember to stop himself in these seven situations? They decide that, with the exception of kicking the seat in the car, the other situations don't really lend themselves to posting a reminder.

The therapist then tells Connor that the reminder card is a cue that helps him remember what to do. He gives Connor the card that says "Don't Do It (kick Mom's seat)" along with a piece of tape and asks that when he leaves, he tape it to the back of the front seat in his mom's car to remind him not to kick.

Holding up the other six cards, the therapist says that taping up cards is one kind of cue, but it's not the only kind. There are lots of other kinds of cues to use as reminders. He will help Connor set up some other cues for the situations on the other cards, but first they will play a game.

Playing games accomplishes several things. First, it provides a context for assessing Connor's level of assisted development—what kinds of assistance help him to improve his performance. Second, play gives the opportunity to learn by doing. It will be much easier for Connor to carry out a home assignment using a skill that he has actually demonstrated, rather than a skill that he has just talked about.

> The therapist leads Connor and his mother through a game of Red Light, Green Light (see Activity 10.3). After having fun with these games, the therapist compliments Connor on his ability to stop himself immediately each time he heard the words "Red light." He explains that those words were a cue for Connor to stop doing something, just like the Don't Do It card.
>
> He gives Connor and Ginger the remaining six cards and asks that they sort them into two groups: easier to change and harder to change, according to how much difficulty Connor would have inhibiting or interrupting his response in each situation. They place "teasing his sisters after being asked to stop," "lying about brushing his teeth," and "talking too loudly in church" in the easier category. The other three—"arguing about bedtime," "getting mad and stomping off when things don't go his way," and "begging his parents to buy him something in the store"—go into the harder category.

Activity 10.3. Red Light, Green Light

RATIONALE: To be successful in many activities, children need to be able to interrupt ongoing responses that are not pertinent or appropriate for a situation.

BENEFIT: As the child demonstrates this ability within the structure of a game, he becomes aware that he can make a conscious choice to interrupt responses. A secondary benefit is that, since the child responds to a verbal cue (the words "Red light"), the same cue can be used by a parent or teacher in other situations in which the child needs to interrupt responses.

MATERIALS NEEDED: None. A large room or long hallway is needed to have sufficient room for the standard play. However, see Variations (below) for ways to play in a smaller space.

EXPLANATION FOR CHILD: Remember that sometimes what you don't do is just as important as what you do. In this assignment, you have to switch from *do* to *don't do* whenever you hear a special cue. The cue to switch from *do* to *don't do* is the words "Red light."

In this game, one person is the stoplight and stands at one end of the room (or hall). The other players stand at the opposite end. When the stoplight says, "Green light," the players can walk, hop on one foot, jump, skip, or crawl (no running unless played outdoors) toward the stoplight. At any time, the stoplight can say, "Red light." Then the players have to stop exactly where they are, even in midmovement. If they move at all after red light is called, they have to go back to the beginning. Then the stoplight says "Green light" and the players can move again until the next time red light is called. The first player to get to the stoplight is the winner and that player becomes the stoplight.

VARIATIONS:
1. The players engage in some sort of activity, such as eating a snack, building with blocks, or putting together a puzzle. They begin when the stoplight says, "Green light" and must stop

(continued)

Activity 10.3. Continued

immediately when they hear the cue "Red light." Since there is no clear end point in this game, just play for a while and when the child shows mastery, switch roles.

2. Make the game more challenging (and silly) by substituting similar-sounding words for "Green light" and "Red light" (e.g., green grass, green tight, red bed, red fight).

EXPAND THIS ACTIVITY: Parents might also try using this same technique at home while the child is performing simple chores (such as setting the table, feeding the dog, folding the clothes). Here's how:
  • Make the green light times longer.
  • When the parent says "Red light," the child must inhibit all action.
  • Use the pause to recognize what the child has done thus far in completing the chore. Express appreciation in specific ways: "Max is a lucky dog to have you to help take care of him. . . . I like the way you put the dog food back on the shelf so neatly. . . . You carried Max's water bowl very carefully."
  • Give a big "Yahoo!" when the chore is done.

Adapted from **Simon Says Pay Attention** (Red Light, Green Light assignment), **p. 71,** © **Golden Path Games, 2009.**

The therapist is sequencing interventions, beginning with problems that are most amenable to change. It is important to assign interventions that are likely to be successful, build on those successes, and work up to more challenging behaviors.

The therapist keeps the "harder to change" cards and gives the three "easier to change" cards to Ginger. He asks if she

would be willing to be Connor's coach and give him a cue—
maybe the words "Red light"—when she notices that he
needs to stop doing any of the things on those cards. She
says that she would be happy to do so. The therapist next
asks Connor if he thinks he could do the same thing at
home or at church that he did today in the game: stop immediately when he gets a cue from his mother. Connor says
that he could.

The therapist writes down their assignment and they decide to stick with the cue "Red light," which Ginger will say
very quietly to Connor when the occasion calls for it. He
asks Ginger to keep track, on the assignment page, of the
number of times she gives the cue and how Connor responds. He also reminds them that when they played the
game Simon Says Don't Do It, he had used the cue "Remember what to say" to help Connor both inhibit his behavior
and use self-talk to help himself stop. He suggests that Ginger might want to use that cue as well, if Connor seemed to
need extra help.

Ginger has two cues that have already been used with Connor to try out at home. Putting the assignment in writing and
asking Ginger to track their progress gives structure to the
assignment.

Both parents attend the next session and Ginger reports on
their assignment. She recorded that she gave the "Red light"
cue 12 times. (She admits that probably twice that number
went unrecorded.) They actually made a new type of cue
card, with a picture of a red light, to use in church as a silent reminder. She reports that the cues worked perfectly
when Connor was being disruptive in church and when he
lied about brushing his teeth. When he teased his sisters,

she sometimes had to add the second cue "Remember what to tell yourself." That usually did the trick, although two times he had become angry with her and she had to put him in time out.

Home assignments fill two purposes: to improve performance in real-life situations, but also to be a kind of ongoing dynamic assessment, providing valuable information about Connor's level of assisted performance. In reviewing this assignment with the family, the therapist learned that (1) Connor was able to respond to the red light cue and stop his behavior when he was not emotionally upset (being disruptive in church, lying about brushing his teeth); and (2) when he was not able to stop his behavior (all occasions related to teasing his sisters), he was emotionally upset. If it was minor teasing and they just wanted him to stop, he was able to do so, but if he was teasing them because he was already upset about something else, he was unable to stop and had to go to time out.

This new information helps the therapist understand the contexts in which Connor may need additional scaffolding. He knows that of the situations they identified in the previous session, the remaining three are also likely to be emotionally charged. Therefore, prior to attempting to intervene directly in these behaviors, the therapist will want more scaffolding. He introduces the concept of shifting focus, building on response inhibition and adding skills for self-calming and cognitive flexibility.

The therapist congratulates Connor on carrying out the previous assignment and for all of his success in stopping himself from doing the wrong thing. He also thanks Connor and his parents for explaining the circumstances when the red light cue wasn't enough help. Now he knows that maybe Connor needs a different kind of help when he is upset.

He explains that he knows Connor wants to do the right thing. "When we feel upset about something, that upset feeling isn't just in our brain, it's in our bodies as well. Our hearts might beat fast, our muscles might feel tense. Our bodies are upset. So even if we are thinking, 'I need to stop,' if we don't calm down our bodies we might not be able to stop."

The therapist next reminds Connor of his first session at the office, when he was feeling nervous. They talk about how the therapist showed Connor how to do an air angel. At first Connor's feeling of nervousness was rated 7, but after doing the air angel and stretching and breathing, he right away felt a bit calmer—a 5.

Therapist: Connor, do you remember how you felt at the end of the session, when you were leaving? What number did you give to your nervous feeling then?

Connor: Just a 2.

Therapist: What did we do during that meeting, between when your feeling was a 5 and when it was a 2?

Connor: We talked about stuff and . . . we played some games. We had fun!

Therapist: That's right. You started off at a 7 and then you did some air angels and that brought it down to a 5. Then you started doing things and talking about things and that brought it down to just a 2. Which feeling did you like best? The 7 or the 5 or the 2?

Connor: Definitely the 2.

Therapist: Breathing, stretching, thinking, talking, doing. Those were all things that helped you calm down and feel less nervous. You did pretty good, don't you think?

Connor: Yeah.

This is another example of sequencing. The therapist is building on Connor's previous success in regulating his emotions. He is also being very specific about the actions that allowed Connor to make this shift. He is helping Connor begin to identify these actions as strategies that can be used in other situations to achieve similar results.

Therapist: Connor, do you know what a tool is?

Connor: Yeah, like a hammer or a saw.

Therapist: Right, and what do tools do for us?

Connor: Um . . . you can build things with them?

Therapist: Exactly. Tools are things that help us to get the job done. A saw and a hammer help you get the job done when you want to build something. It would be a lot harder to build something without a hammer and a saw, wouldn't it?

Connor: Yeah, a lot harder.

Therapist: So, if you have the right tools, the job is a lot easier. Now a saw and a hammer are tools that we can see. Did you know that there are tools that we can't see?

Connor: Invisible tools?

Therapist: Well, kind of. A tool is anything that makes it easier to get a job done. Like when you did the air angel and your nervous feeling went from a 7 down to a 5. The air angel was a tool that you used to do the job of calming yourself down.

Mediators provide a way to turn over responsibility for regulating their behavior to the children themselves. The air angel is a mediator—the mental image provides a structure that guides the child through the actions involved in self-calming—deep breathing and muscle relaxation. The therapist is setting the stage for introducing another mediator as a home assignment.

Therapist: You did a great job with the air angel, so I am going to give you another tool that you can use to calm yourself down when you are nervous or angry or upset. Okay?

Connor: Okay.

Therapist: Hmm. . . . How should I teach you about the tool? Do you want a 1-hour PowerPoint lecture or should we play a game?

Connor: A game!

Therapist: Good choice! The name of the game is Stop, Relax, Focus, Go!

The therapist introduces the activity Stop, Relax, Focus, Go! (Activity 10.4). In this game, the stop sign is a mediator; it will

---

Activity 10.4. Stop, Relax, Focus, Go!

RATIONALE: Many children have difficulty with shifting focus, including (1) the cognitive and behavioral flexibility that enables them to calm down when overly excited or upset, (2) the ability to consider events from multiple viewpoints, and (3) the ability to transition smoothly from one set of circumstances to another.

BENEFIT: This activity raises the child's awareness that he can utilize specific strategies to prepare for shifting focus. This activity also introduces the idea of using a stop sign as a visual cue to initiate these strategies.

MATERIALS NEEDED:
1. A stop sign (purchase at an educational supply store or make your own).

(continued)

Activity 10.4. Continued

2. Materials for two different ball games (or materials for two other games; see Variation below):
   • A soft ball to throw
   • A basket or container in which to throw the ball
   • A writing board or piece of paper for recording names and scores.

EXPLANATION FOR CHILD:
1. In today's activity you have to be able to switch your focus (or switch gears). That means you quickly and completely stop one game and get ready to start another.
   • *Quickly* means that you stop the first game as soon as you get the signal to stop.
   • *Completely* means that you won't even think about that first game anymore. You'll focus all of your attention on the new game. Even if you were having fun with the first game, you'll just let go of it and focus on the new game.
2. It's not always easy to stop doing something, so to help us make the switch, we are going to use this stop sign as a reminder of how to switch gears. We can use three things to help us switch, and the three things all start with the letter B.
   a. We can use our Breath: Taking a deep breath helps us calm down and get ready to focus on something new.
   b. We can use our Body: Paying attention to our muscles and relaxing any that are tight or tense helps us calm down and get ready to focus on something new.
   c. We can use our Brain: Saying the right things to ourselves helps us focus on what we need to do.

3. Let's practice. (Note: Do each step along with the child, going slowly and modeling the proper technique.)
   First, let's just look at the stop sign.
   Next, let's take a good, long, deep breath.
   Next, let's pay attention to our bodies, and relax any muscles that feel tight or tense.
   And last—but not least—let's make sure our brains are sending us the right message.

I'm going to have my brain say, "Calm down and get ready to focus on the new game." What are you going to have your brain say?

INSTRUCTIONS:

Today's activity is called Stop, Relax, Focus, Go! We will have to switch between two different games:

Game 1: The Ball Toss Game

Game 2: The First Annual World Championship Indoor Nerf Basketball Game.

For the Ball Toss Game, we just toss the ball back and forth, like this. But for the First Annual World Championship Basketball Game, we become world-famous NBA basketball players. Let's decide who we want to be and I'll write our names on this Official World Championship Game Scoreboard. (Decide on names, giving the child help if needed. Write both names on the board.) When we are world-famous NBA players, we have to throw the ball in this Official Championship Game Goal. When we make it, we get a point on the scoreboard. We'll each get a practice shot right now.

Okay, here's how we play Stop, Relax, Focus, Go!
- We start with Game 1, just tossing the ball back and forth.
- Whenever I say "Stop," we have to switch to Game 2 and become champion basketball players.
- We'll make the switch by doing what we practiced. We will look at the stop sign and
  1. Take a deep breath
  2. Relax our muscles
  3. Focus our thinking on the new game

(Note: The therapist should fully demonstrate all the steps below, and also model internalized speech by thinking aloud while going through each step.)

1. Begin with Game 1 (just tossing the ball back and forth).
2. When the therapist says "Stop," the player with the ball stops tossing the ball and focuses on a bright red stop sign on the wall. (Internalized speech: "I'm stopping the Ball Toss Game. I am looking at the stop sign and I'm not even going to think about the Ball Toss Game any more.")

(continued)

Activity 10.4. Continued

3. When the therapist says "Relax," the player takes a deep breath and relaxes his body. (Internalized speech: "I'm taking a slow, deep breath to get ready for the new game. I'm checking my body to make sure I'm relaxed and ready to focus on the new game.")

4. When the therapist says "Focus," the player turns to the basketball goal and focuses his eyes and mind on the new activity. (Internalized speech: "I'm thinking just about the new game now. I'm focusing on being a basketball player and doing my best.")

5. When the therapist says "Go!" the player throws the ball to the basket. (Internalized speech: "I made it!" or "I didn't make it, but that was a good effort." "I'm getting a little better each time." "I'll have another chance in a little while.")

6. The player's score is recorded and then the Ball Toss Game resumes until the therapist calls "Stop."

Continue for several rounds. Make it fun, but be sure to emphasize the steps involved in switching focus: stopping on cue, relaxing completely, and focusing thoughts on the new activity.

VARIATION: In the instructions above, the players switch between two different ball games. However, you can use any two games or activities that have high appeal for the child.

Adapted from **Simon Says Pay Attention** (Stop, Relax, Focus, Go! activity), **p. 88,** © **Golden Path Games, 2009.**

---

later be incorporated into a new home assignment. As he carries out this activity, the therapist explains slowly and carefully what to do when looking at the stop sign. He wants to be sure that Connor is able to do all of the parts involved in shifting focus: breathing deeply, relaxing any muscle tension, and using private speech to enhance cognitive flexibility. In the office, Connor repeats the activity three times, once with the therapist and once with each parent.

Next, the therapist gives a new home assignment. Connor is instructed to make a stop sign poster to use at home to practice his Stop, Relax, Focus, Go! skills. This poster will be a tool that will help him remember all the parts involved in calming down and shifting focus. The therapist gives him a handout that he can simply decorate and use (Figure 10.2). If he wants to make his own poster, the therapist tells him, it needs to have a stop sign and some kind of words or pictures to remind him of the actions he needs to take (deep breathing and muscle relaxation) and the things that he can tell himself (private speech).

Next, the therapist involves the parents as facilitators in this assignment. He wants to sequence the use of this mediator so that Connor experiences success; therefore he wants to use it initially when Connor has to shift focus in some way, but not when he is emotionally upset. Only after Connor shows that he can use this tool in the new context (at home, when he has to transition between activities) will the therapist ask that he use it for more challenging situations.

Therapist: Jason and Ginger, can I get your help again as coaches for Connor's new assignment?

Jason and Ginger: Yes.

Therapist: After Connor makes his stop sign poster, I want you to have him practice using it 10 times before his next appointment. He'll use it the same way that we played the game today, to stop thinking about what he is already doing and to start thinking about the next thing he is going to do.

I want you to choose the times that he'll practice. Choose times when you want him to stop doing one thing and start doing something else, for example, when it is time to stop watching TV and start getting ready for bed. Or when it is

FIGURE 10.2. Stop and Think poster.

time to stop playing and start doing homework. Or when it is time to stop reading a book and start helping you fix dinner. Any questions?

Ginger: Yes. What if he doesn't do what we tell him to do?

Therapist: Good question! I am going to ask you to keep score on this card.

The score card (Figure 10.3) will also serve as a mediator, helping to track Connor's progress in using this tool in the home context. The therapist is setting up as much external support as he thinks Connor may need. The therapist could have provided more external support by linking a reward to completion of the assignment—for example, allowing Connor

FIGURE 10.3. Cue card and score card.

to earn points that he could then exchange for prizes from the office "treasure chest."

Therapist: There are 10 spaces on this card, one for each time that you give Connor the instruction to use the stop sign. If he uses his poster and switches to the new activity, give him a check in that space. If he doesn't use his poster or doesn't switch to the new activity, put an X in that space. Next time you come, I'll look and see how many checks Connor earned. Connor, how many checks do you think you will earn?

Connor: I think 10.

Therapist: That would be great! You did a really good job here today, so I know that you know what to do. But it might not be as easy to do it at home. That's what we are going to find out with this assignment—is it as easy to do at home as it was here? Or will it be harder at home? If it's too hard, we'll think of a way to help you out. If it's easy, well, that will mean you may be ready for an even bigger challenge!

The therapist is defining the home assignment not as a pass-fail test but as a way of gathering information, of understanding Connor's level of assisted development. He is also letting them know that the assignments will be an ongoing process and he is getting a feel for how willing they are to do the work that will be required of all of them.

Jason: If there is one thing that Connor is good at, it is meeting challenges. He is a hard worker when he puts his mind to something. We've been practicing for his baseball games and he wears me out—I think he could keep on practicing forever.

Therapist: That's good to hear. And Connor, the more you practice with your stop sign poster, the better you will be at calming yourself down and switching gears when you need to. I'm looking forward to hearing what happens at home.

Connor's parents are committed to helping him overcome the impulsiveness that is causing him so much difficulty socially. (When the therapist later commends them on how much time they put in on this, Jason comments that they devote much more time to Connor's ball games and that self-control is far more important than athletic skills. He has good insight into the amount of time and effort required for behavioral change to take place.) When they return for their next appointment, Connor has indeed received 10 checks.

Over the next several months, the assignments are tweaked, with Connor gradually beginning to use the stop poster as a mediator. Connor and his parents make some mini stop sign posters that they keep in the car or in a pocket for occasions when they are away from home.

Over time, the parents report that Connor has begun to occasionally use the stop sign when he is upset without needing a reminder. The therapist makes a big deal out of this, congratulating Connor on using his self-calming tools on his own. This is indeed a milestone because it means that Connor is using his working memory to remind himself of his intentions and goals; he needs less scaffolding to be able to recognize the need to inhibit a response. The parents are still concerned about Connor's social skills, so the therapist also teaches them how to hold family meetings at home. The communication and problem-solving skills used in the family meeting will help Connor practice age-appropriate social skills that he may have failed to acquire previously because of his impulsivity.

At a session about 7 months after the start of therapy, Connor tells the therapist about a time that he stopped and calmed himself down when he was by himself.

Connor: I was at baseball practice, and I got really mad because my glove wasn't on the bleachers where I left it. I thought that Jackson took it, because he is always taking people's stuff. I was so mad, I wanted to hit him. I don't like people using my glove.

Therapist: So, you were feeling so mad you wanted to hit Jackson. What happened next?

Connor: I started to walk over to where Jackson was. But I used my stop sign and calmed myself down.

Therapist: Oh, did you have your mini stop sign in your pocket?

Connor: No, I didn't have it. So I used the one in my head.

Therapist: Wow! You have one in your head now? How did that work?

Connor: Good. I calmed down and I stopped going over there.

Therapist: What happened next?

Connor: I remembered that I left my glove on the other bleachers. I went over there and looked and it was still there.

Therapist: So Jackson hadn't taken it after all?

Connor: Nope.

Therapist: That's fantastic, Connor. You used your head and calmed yourself down and solved the problem.

Connor has internalized the stop sign mediator and used that internalized image to help him inhibit his initial response and then think more flexibly about the situation. The therapist celebrates this event with Connor as a big step toward gaining the ability to control his impulses on his own, without so much outside help. Shortly after this session, there is an opportunity for Connor to join a social skills group for boys his age. Connor, his parents, and the therapist discuss this and decide that Connor is ready for the group. Connor's experience with internalizing a mediator makes them all feel confident that, although neither his current therapist nor a parent will be there to monitor him, he is now much more able to monitor his own behavior, control his reactions, and thus benefit from the group instruction and interaction. They make plans to terminate, for now, Connor's individual therapy.

After termination, the therapist still runs into Connor because the group sessions are held at the same office. He has the opportunity to observe Connor in the waiting room and notes that he is well liked by the other boys in the group. The group therapist confirms that Connor is doing well in the group, and Ginger and Jason report that he is spending more time with his old friends and is again being included in outings and sleepovers.

Summary

- Problem: Nine-year-old Connor is having difficulty in almost all social situations because of impulsive behavior, including some angry and aggressive behavior.
- Goal: Connor will have a better understanding of his problem with impulse control. He will (1) learn strategies for response inhibition, and (2) work with his parents to implement plans for using those strategies at the point of performance.
- Facilitators: Connor's therapist and parents acted as facilitators.
- Dynamic assessment: The facilitators observed and created contexts for assessing Connor's level of assisted performance: the feelings poster, Don't Do It cards, Simon Says Don't Do It game, Red Light, Green Light activity, and the Stop, Relax, Focus, Go! activity.
- Point-of-performance interventions: Don't Do It cards taped on the TV; Connor's mother saying "Red light" as a cue to

inhibit actions; a stop sign poster, with a score card to monitor the practice; using the stop sign poster at home as a mediator; using a mini stop sign outside the home to scaffold self-calming; and using a mental stop sign.

- Other interventions: family meetings and social skills group.
- Results: Connor truly became an active partner in managing his difficulty with response inhibition. These types of problem behaviors are frequently managed by complicated behavioral contingency programs (e.g., charting, systems of positive and negative reinforcers) administered by adults, or by use of medication. Because both Connor and his parents were highly motivated to use strategies that placed more responsibility on Connor himself, they were able to forego both of these approaches. This took a lot of time and hard work on everyone's part, but the family was very pleased with the results.

CHAPTER ELEVEN

Jon, Age 10, Fifth Grade

Executive Functions Involved: Working Memory

Working memory refers to brain processes that temporarily store, organize, and manipulate information. Working memory enables us to hold several pieces of information in mind while we try to do something with them—for example, solve a problem or carry out a task. Working memory is closely related to internalized language. Some children, particularly those with attention problems, may have delays in this process of internalizing speech and may not use self-directed language as effectively as others of the same age.

Working memory is important for following instructions in school as well as in everyday tasks. Because it underlies and contributes to the other executive functions, children with working memory deficits will appear to have poor response inhibition (if they can't recall what they are supposed to be doing, they are likely to react to whatever most immediately captures their attention). Goal orientation will also be compromised (once a plan is made, working memory is needed to stay on track toward the completion of the plan). Children who are delayed in working memory and internalized language may perform very well in situations where they respond primarily to external sources of information (e.g., a class discussion or a group project) but will have difficulty when they are on their own and need to rely on internally represented information to guide their own performance.

Summary of Previous Interventions

Ten-year-old Jon is far behind his peers in his ability to hold information in mind and to reliably initiate actions that are part of his daily routine: getting ready for school, completing homework, and doing tasks and chores around the house.

When Jon was in the second grade, he was diagnosed with ADHD. He was placed on medication for a short time, but his mother, Mia, decided to stop it due to side effects. Instead, each year his teachers have made accommodations: placing Jon near their desks, assigning a buddy to help him check his book sack before going home, and keeping Mia in the loop by signing off on his daily assignment pad and sending frequent e-mails. However, now that he is in the fifth grade, some of the supports are less available. Although Jon is performing acceptably at school and is well liked by his teachers and classmates, he is often forgetful about assignments and even about things that he looks forward to.

In addition to facing the challenges at school, Mia has become increasingly frustrated with Jon's inability to follow through on instructions at home, such as getting ready for a trip, preparing for school in the morning, and completing homework assignments in the afternoon. Mia has begun to worry that he is slipping too far behind his peers. He seems increasingly immature in comparison to his friends.

After discussing her concerns with the school counselor, Mia received a referral to a therapist, where she and Jon discuss her concerns. In Chapters 1 and 2, we discussed the details of the first therapy session in which the therapist:

1. Had them play the game Ready, Set, Go For It.
2. Introduced a definition of working memory as "holding things in mind so you can do the right thing at the right time."
3. Gave Jon a home assignment to use a wrist list to do his chores on the following Saturday. The assignment created a context in which the therapist could assess Jon's willingness and ability to use external support for his working memory.

Mental Health Clinician's Role

Mia is already providing extensive scaffolding for Jon. The clinician helps them plan a way for Mia to scale back on the scaffolding and for Jon to take on more responsibility for strengthening, and providing external support for, his working memory.

This is fairly short-term therapy, using just three interventions (wrist list, Stay-on-Track Map, and Encouraging Words cue cards) that demonstrate ways that Jon can become more self-directed. However, although the therapy itself is short term, the end result is that Mia (and to some extent Jon himself) develops an accurate, long-term vision of Jon's developmental needs.

When Jon and Mia return for their second session, the therapist reviews the assignment and finds that it was very successful. Jon was enthusiastic about doing the assignment and was able to recall his regular chores and list them with minimal help from Mia. He then carried out all of the steps without any reminders from her.

The therapist cannot assume that, because Jon provided his own scaffolding in doing his chores, he will now transfer this skill to new situations. Jon needs to "own" his problem and to make a commitment to using strategies to compensate for it. At the second session, the therapist requests that he come up with a plan to provide his own scaffolding for a situation that may be more challenging.

Therapist: Since you did so well using the wrist list as a memory helper, let's try using a memory helper for another situation where you have trouble staying on track.

Mia: I'd really like to find a way for Jon to stay on track in the morning. He's old enough that he should be able to get ready for school on his own, without me always having to be on top of him.

Therapist: Okay. Let me make sure I understand what is needed. Jon, what are the things that you need to do in the morning to get ready for school?

Jon: Um . . . eat breakfast. And feed Max. I get Max's food ready while Mom is getting my food ready.

Therapist: Okay. Then after breakfast, what's next?

Jon: I have to go upstairs and get ready.

Therapist: What does that mean?

Jon: Get dressed, brush my teeth, comb my hair.

Therapist: Then what's next?

Jon: Then I'm ready to go.

Mia: And get your book sack.

Jon: Oh, yeah, get my book sack and then meet Pierre and go to the bus.

Jon is able to recall almost all of the things that he needs to do. The problem is not that he doesn't know, or can't remember, what to do. It is that he does not reliably retrieve this information at the point of performance. Currently, he is relying on his mother to help him retrieve this information. The therapist next helps Jon and Mia make a plan for transferring this responsibility to Jon.

Therapist: So, Mia, it looks like Jon knows all of the things he is supposed to do in the morning, right?

Mia: Yes. He obviously does. I wish he'd just do them.

Therapist: Right now, he gets those things done on time, but only because you, Mia, keep giving him cues, or reminders, to move on to the next thing. That keeps him on track, right?

Mia: Right. I'm his memory helper right now.

Therapist: If there were a way for Jon to give himself the cue, then you wouldn't have to be his memory helper any more, right?

Mia: Hmm. That sounds like I'm being kind of lazy. It's not really that much work to tell him what to do.

Therapist: No, it is important for Jon to be able to remind himself, because you can't always be there to remind him, right?

Change is difficult for everyone, even for the parents who are requesting the change. The external support that Mia put in place has given them peace in the morning and she probably has some anxiety about anything that would disrupt that peace. The therapist reminds Mia that their goal is not just to get Jon ready for school in the morning, but to help Jon achieve greater independence. The therapist is keeping Mia focused on the long-term vision and the benefits that will come with removing some of her scaffolding.

Mia: Absolutely. You are right. Jon is a great kid, and I want him to be able to grow up to be a responsible person. I want him to be able to get things done on his own so he can feel proud of himself and other people can depend on him.

Therapist: I agree. Jon, your mom has been your memory helper in the morning. Would you like to try an experiment and see if you can use a different memory helper in the morning—something to remind you to do the right thing at the right time?

Jon: Maybe I could do a wrist list in the morning.

Therapist: That's an idea, but you already know how to use that memory helper, so let's try a different one this time. I'm thinking of a memory helper that I call the Stay-on-Track Map.

The therapist wants to try out several mediators, partly to see which ones are effective but also to help Jon understand that he has multiple options to support his working memory. She helps Jon create a visual map of what he needs to do in the morning (Figure 11.1). Over the next couple of sessions, they fine tune his use of the Stay-on-Track Map. For example, at the next session, the therapist learns that the map has been successful on some days, but not if Jon leaves it on the kitchen table when he goes upstairs. In response, she explains the concept of point of performance. After some discussion, they decide to make multiple copies of the map and place one at the kitchen table, one on Jon's bedroom door, and one on the bathroom mirror so that there is a reminder at each point of performance. The therapist also begins to the address the issue of internalized language. The therapist suspects that Jon is not using internalized language effectively, so she also encourages him to state his intentions aloud as

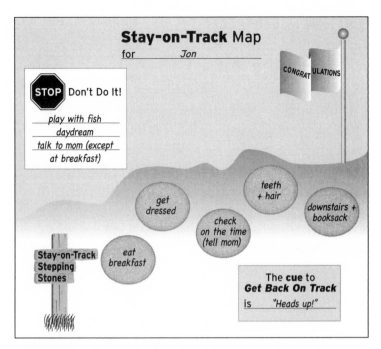

FIGURE 11.1. Jon's Stay-on-Track map.

he moves from one step to the next on his Stay-on-Track map.

The therapist continues the emphasis on internalized language when they turn their attention to a third problem area: completing homework. The therapist knows from previous discussions that Jon begins his homework after dinner and that it takes "forever" to complete. He does it at the kitchen table as Mia cleans up after their supper and does other chores. Typically, Jon tries to engage Mia in conversation and she tries to redirect him to his assignments. He usually complains a bit ("It's too hard," "It's too much," "I don't really need to know this because . . .") and often tries to talk his mother into letting him watch TV or play a game first. His mother has to keep bringing him back to the task at hand. He usually finishes his homework just before bedtime and sometimes must finish in the morning before he goes to school. During the school week, Jon rarely watches TV (or plays on the computer or plays a board game with his mother), because he has rarely completed his homework in time to earn those privileges. Jon expresses unhappiness over this, but Mia points out that it is up to him. He can have all of those privileges whenever he wants them—he just has to get his homework done.

Jon does not seem to use speech effectively to guide his behavior. He talks a lot, but his speech is more social: Its focus is external, not internal. The therapist suspects that his inner speech is not task oriented, and in fact might be task resistant. She wants to help Jon learn to use internalized speech more effectively. She decides to give him an assignment of using cue cards to guide his private speech during homework. First, however, she engages him in an activity to help him be more aware of how he is currently using internalized language.

Therapist: On a scale of 1 to 10, how badly do you want to get your homework done so you can watch TV?

Jon: Definitely a 10.

Therapist: So, if I understand you, every day you have a goal of getting your homework done and watching TV. I know that at soccer, you're pretty good at getting your goals. But when it comes to getting this goal, you hardly ever get it. I wonder why that is.

Jon: I have no idea.

party is on Saturday, and when I am going to take him to get a present. Oh, and he told me about his coach fussing at some of the boys at practice.

The therapist continues writing these sentences on cards and placing them in front of Jon.

Therapist: Jon, what do you think to yourself while you are doing your homework?

Jon: I just think about my homework.

Therapist: Mia, can you guess what Jon might be thinking?

Mia: Well, sometimes Jon complains that it is too much work or it is too hard.

Therapist: Okay. I'll write those down. Jon, we are about to play a game with these cards, and the more of your thoughts we have down, the better. Let's see if you can think of one more thing that you sometimes tell yourself while you are working on your homework.

Jon: Sometimes I think that I hate school.

They now have a stack of 10 cards representing the type of speech that Jon typically uses during homework time.

Therapist: Now we are ready to play the game. In a minute I am going to ask you to read each sentence out loud. But first, I need to explain how words can be tools. The wrist list is a tool that helps you stay on track and get your chores done. The Stay-on-Track map is a tool that helps you get ready in the morning. The right words can be tools that encourage you to get your homework done so you can watch TV.

So here's the game. You are going to read each card out loud and decide if the words are a good tool—do they encourage you to get your homework done so you can watch TV? If they are a good tool, put the card back down on the floor in

Therapist: You did great with the wrist list and the Stay-on-Track Map. Those were tools that you used all by yourself to help you meet your goals. Would you be willing to try a tool to help yourself meet your goal of getting your homework done and watching TV?

The therapist is building on Jon's previous success and reminding him of the long-term vision of his being more independent and self-directed. For the next intervention, she, Jon, and Mia sit on the floor with a stack of blank index cards and a pencil.

Therapist: One way to help yourself meet a goal is to pay careful attention to what you tell yourself. When you sit down at the table to do your homework, what is the first thing that you usually tell yourself?
Jon: I don't say anything.
Therapist: Mia, what have you noticed that Jon talks about when he first sits down to do his homework?
Mia: A lot of the time he asks me if he can please watch TV first, even though he knows I'll say no.
Therapist: Jon, when your mom says no, do you think to yourself that she's being mean or that it's not fair?
Jon: Yeah. I don't say it, but maybe I think it's not fair.
Therapist: Okay. I'm going to write "It's not fair!" on this card.

The therapist writes this sentence on an index card and places it in front of Jon. She is externalizing his thought processes for him, so he will be able to see what he commonly tells himself.

Therapist: Mia, what else do you notice that Jon talks about while he is doing his homework?
Mia: Well, yesterday he asked me what time Sam's birthday

front of you. If they are not a good tool scrunch the card up and toss it into the trash can over there.

Jon enjoyed reading each one—and scrunching it up and throwing it in the trash. In the end he was left with a blank floor. This was a very concrete demonstration of the fact that his speech—both externalized and internalized—was not encouraging him to reach his goal.

Therapist: Okay, the next part of this game is to make 10 new cards—cards that will be good tools. That means 10 things that you can say to encourage yourself to reach your goal.

Jon, Mia, and the therapist spend 10 minutes brainstorming for ideas, and Jon writes them on the cards (Figure 11.2). Each card contains one sentence:

The therapist next gives Jon and Mia an assignment using the cue cards. The assignment takes place in two stages, with Mia initially providing scaffolding to help Jon use the cue cards properly. In the second stage, Mia is to cut back on the amount of scaffolding, turning more responsibility over to Jon.

> The therapist explains that in the first stage, Mia will act as Jon's coach when he sits down at the table to begin his homework. Unlike Jon's soccer coach, she is going to be a silent coach. Every few minutes, Mia is to select a cue card and put it in front of Jon. Jon should then read the card aloud. If Jon asks Mia any unrelated questions, she is to ignore them. In fact, because Jon rarely needs help with the content of his homework, Mia is to ignore any questions that Jon asks. Her only job will be to choose the cue card that she thinks has the best words for Jon to encourage himself to reach his goal.

FIGURE 11.2. Jon's cue cards.

The therapist also gives Jon and Mia some blank cards so they can add more sentences as they work on this plan. She suggests another sentence and writes it down: "If my mom ignores me, that is a cue to get back to work."

The therapist gives instructions for the second stage of the assignment, to begin after they have followed Stage 1 for a full week. In the second stage, Mia will not choose the card for Jon. Instead, she will remind him every few minutes by ringing a bell. When he hears the bell, Jon is to choose a card on his own and read it aloud.

Before they leave the office, the therapist has Jon and Mia run through a quick practice session to make sure they understand how to use the cards in each stage. They do an excellent job and Jon is excited about the assignment.

Mia has been providing scaffolding by sitting with Jon to keep him on track. This assignment turns that responsibility over to Jon, but in a gradual way. Now the cards provide scaffolding, giving Jon preplanned private speech that he can use to keep himself on track. Currently, his private speech is immature, often off task or discouraging.

When Jon and Mia return in 2 weeks, Jon happily announces that he has been able to watch TV almost every night. Mia expresses surprise at how much faster homework goes now that she is not talking with Jon anymore. She thought that she was helping him stay on track but realizes now that they spent a lot of time arguing about his homework or talking about irrelevant things. Using the cards felt awkward at first, but they like the results, so they have been continuing to do it.

The therapist again emphasizes their long-term goal of independence for Jon. It's great that he is able to watch TV, but even greater that he has learned lots of strategies for keeping himself on track. She now wants to tweak the assignment again and remove more of Mia's scaffolding.

The therapist asks them to continue the cue card assignment for another 2 weeks, and asks them to think of ways to turn more responsibility over to Jon. They discuss what will happen if Mia leaves the room and Jon is completely on his own. Both Mia and Jon are concerned that he might fall back into old habits, and lose out on watching TV. They decide that Mia should stay in the room and read a book, but instead of Mia ringing a bell, Jon will use a timer to remind himself to read a card, setting it for 3-minute intervals.

When they return for their next session, they report that their plan has worked well. The only help that Mia now provides during homework is her physical presence in the room. They discuss Jon's progress in providing his own memory helpers. He continues to use the wrist list on chore days. He has his Stay-on-Track Maps posted in three places, and most days he is able to complete his morning routine with only an occasional reminder from Mia. He has the cue cards at the kitchen table to remind himself to use language to keep himself on track.

Jon and Mia have two additional sessions, which they use primarily to review Jon's progress and to establish a long-term vision for continuing to support Jon's development in coming years. The therapist helps them to recognize that Jon may always have difficulties with working memory, but now they each know what they can do to help. Mia knows that one of the most important ways that she can help Jon is to help him figure out ways to help himself. And Jon knows that he has a number of tools to use in situations where his working memory is weak. First, he can use mediators like the wrist list and the Stay-on-Track Map. Second, he can pay attention to what he tells himself inside his head and be sure that he is saying things that will encourage him to keep his goal in mind.

Summary

- Problem: Ten-year-old Jon fails to fulfill daily expectations at home. His mother has to provide extensive external support for him to do the right thing at the right time.
- Goal: Jon will acquire strategies for providing himself with the external support that he needs to get routine tasks done.
- Facilitators: Jon's mother, Mia, had been facilitating his performance with a great deal of scaffolding. However, whenever she reduced the scaffolding, Jon's performance slipped back to where it was before. In this example, Jon learns to facilitate his own performance by using self-directed strategies.
- Dynamic assessment: The Ready, Set, Go for It! game created a context in which Jon could test his working memory and learn about using mediators to provide external support. In the first session, the therapist assigned the wrist list, which created a context of assistance from a mediator. Next, the cue card activity at the therapist's office provided a context for assessing Jon's internalized language.
- Point-of-performance interventions: The wrist list, the Stay-on-Track Map, and the Encouraging Words cue cards.
- Other interventions and amplification: Mia was referred to a support group for parents of children with ADHD to continue to learn more about executive functions.
- Results: Jon was already performing well due to the scaffolding Mia was providing. The main purpose of therapy was to teach Jon self-directed strategies to plan, monitor, and guide his own performance. They succeeded in doing this.

Conclusion

WE HOPE THAT THIS book will inspire other therapists to plan playful, child-friendly interventions to help children improve self-regulation. In planning interventions, we are guided by these essential practices and beliefs.

1) **We help the family view the child's self-regulation problems through the lens of executive function.** The concept of executive function provides a specific focus for intervention. We tell the family that we will work on improving the child's *working memory, response inhibition, cognitive flexibility,* or *goal orientation* and explain the current difficulty in terms of that function.

2) **We engage the child as an active partner in his or her treatment.** All too often treatment for self-regulation is something done to the child or for the child. We make it clear from the beginning that children will be actively involved in understanding and solving their own problems.

3) **We believe that "learning leads development."** Just because a child has not yet developed in keeping with his or her peers, doesn't mean that he or she can't develop or that we have to wait passively for some future maturation to take hold. Carefully planned learning activities, linked

to a specific executive function, can often foster development.

4) **We believe in the therapeutic power of play.** Play engages children in the therapy process. And a carefully planned play intervention can be one of those learning activities that help lead development.

5) **We are ever mindful of the significance of the "point of performance."** Effective interventions are those that can be put in place at the point of performance—the real-life circumstance in which the child is having difficulty with self-regulation. Proper scaffolding allows children to experience success in regulating their thoughts, emotions, and behavior at the exact times that they are having difficulties. Scaffolding can be removed as the child's executive functions develop, or it can be left in place with the child becoming progressively more responsible for providing his or her own scaffolding.

References

Barkley, R. (1997). *ADHD and the nature of self-control.* New York: Guilford.

Barkley, R. (2011). Is executive functioning deficient in ADHD? It depends on your definitions and your measures. The *ADHD Report, 19*(4), pp 1-9, 16.

Berk, L. E. (1994). Why children talk to themselves. *Scientific American, 271*(5), 78–83.

Berk, L. E. (2001). Trends in human development. In J. S. Halonen & S. F. Davis (Eds.), *The many faces of psychological research in the 21ˢᵗ century* (chap. 10). Retrieved from http://teachpsych.org/resources/e-books/faces/index_faces.php

Berk, L. E., Mann, T. D., & Ogan, A. T. (2006). Make-believe play well-spring of self regulation. In D. G. Singer, R. M. Golinkoff, & K. Hirsh-Pasek (Eds.), *Play = learning: How play motivates and enhances children's cognitive and social-emotional growth* (pp. 74–100). New York: Oxford University Press.

Berk, L. E., & Potts, M. K. (1991). Development and functional significance of private speech among attention-deficit hyperactivity disordered and normal boys. *Journal of Abnormal Child Psychology, 19*(3), 357–377.

Best, J. R., Miller, P. H., & Jones, L. I. (2009). Executive functions after age 5: Changes and correlates. *Developmental Review, 29*(3), 180–200.

Bodrova, E., & Leong, D. J. (2005). High quality preschool programs:

What would Vygotsky say? *Early Education and Development,* *16*(4), 437–446.

Bodrova, E., & Leong, D. J. (2007). *Tools of the mind: The Vygotskian approach to early childhood education.* Upper Saddle River, NJ: Pearson Education.

Brown, T. E. (2005). *Attention deficit disorder: The unfocused mind in children and adults.* New Haven, CT: Yale University Press.

Center on the Developing Child. (2011). *Building the brain's "air traffic control" system: How early experiences shape the development of executive function. Working Paper No. 11.* Harvard University. Retrieved from www.developingchild.harvard.edu

Cooper-Kahn, J., & Dietzel, L. (2008). *Late, lost, and unprepared: A parents' guide to helping children with executive functioning.* Betheda, MD: Woodbine House.

Dawson, P., & Guare, R. (2009). *Smart but scattered: The revolutionary "executive skills" approach to helping kids reach their potential.* New York: Guilford.

Diamond, A., Barnett, W. S., Thomas, J., & Munro, S. (2007). Preschool program improves cognitive control. *Science, 318*(5855), 1387–1388.

Diamond, A., & Lee, K. (2011). Interventions shown to aid executive function in children 4 to 12 years old. *Science, 333,* 959–964.

Garon, N., Bryson, S. E., & Smith, I. M. (2008). Executive function in preschoolers: A review using an integrative framework. *Psychological Bulletin, 134*(1), 31–60.

Gawrilow, C., Gollwitzer, P. M., & Oettingen, G. (2011). If-then plans benefit executive functions in children with ADHD. *Journal of Social and Clinical Psychology, 30*(6), 616–646.

Haight, W. L.. & Miller, P.J. (1993). Pretending at home: Early development in a sociocultural context. Albany, NY: State University of New York Press.

Jurado, M. B., & Rosselli, M. (2007). The elusive nature of executive functions: A review of our current understanding. *Neuropsychology Review, 17,* 213–233.

Mischel, W., Shoda, Y., & Rodriguez, M. L. (1989). Delay of gratification in children. *Science, 244,* 933–938.

Miyake, A., Emerson, M. J., Padilla, F., & Ahn, J. (2004). Inner speech as a retrieval aid for task goals: The effects of cue type and articulatory suppression. *Acta Psychologia, 115,* 123–142.

Moffitt, T. E., Arseneault, L., Belsky, D., Dickson, N., Hancox, R., Harrington, H. L., Houts, R., Poulton, R., Roberts, B., Ross, S., Sears, M., Thomson, W. M., & Caspi, A. (2011). A gradient of childhood self-control predicts health, wealth, and public safety. *Proceedings of the National Academy of Sciences, 108,* 2693–2698.

Welsh, M. C., & Pennington, B. F. (1988). Assessing frontal lobe functioning in children: Views from developmental psychology. *Developmental Neuropsychology, 4,* 199–230.

Vygotsky, L. S. (1978). *Mind in society: The development of higher psychological processes.* Cambridge, MA: Harvard University Press.

Yeager, D., & Yeager, M. (2009). *Simon says pay attention: Help for children with ADHD.* Lafayette, LA : Golden Path Games.

Zelazo, P. D., & Paus, T. (2010). Developmental social neuroscience: An introduction. *Social Neuroscience, 5,* 417–421.

Index

In this index, *f* denotes figure and *t* denotes table.